Jacci Smith Reed
11/13/11

A Stranger
in the house

A Stranger
in the house

A journal of my life living the last years with my husband's Alzheimer's

Jacci Smith Reed

Order this book online at www.trafford.com
or email orders@trafford.com

Most Trafford titles are also available at major online book retailers.

Printed in the United States of America.

ISBN: 978-1-4269-9476-0 (sc)
ISBN: 978-1-4269-9475-3 (hc)
ISBN: 978-1-4269-9474-6 (e)

Library of Congress Control Number: 2011916578

Trafford rev. 09/14/2011

 www.trafford.com

North America & international
toll-free: 1 888 232 4444 (USA & Canada)
phone: 250 383 6864 ♦ fax: 812 355 4082

Jacci Smith Reed

We walked a road we did not choose
Our future was unclear
The way was filled with darkness
Sadness, Anger, Fear

It was so hard for me
To watch you die a little more each day
But harder still for you, I guess
You didn't want to be that way

I remember us in a better time
A time for you and me
When life was normal, before you changed
And lost your memory

We walked this journey - You and I
Knowing nothing was "for sure"
And every day I prayed to God
That there would be a cure

I walked this journey with you
We were together til the end
Because I loved you—then and now
And always will—my friend.

In Loving Memory of Ron Reed - May 26th 1932 - October 18th 2003

Contents

Preface

This book began as a daily journal for me, to start to learn, to cope and to survive the misfortunes my husband, Ron, and I had encountered.

I was not prepared for this journey. I did not plan for it and I did not welcome it. I denied it, fought it, hated it, learned about it, accepted it, embraced it and eventually was even thankful for it. It took me years to move forward and it was through my writing that I learned this was not Ron's disease—this was our disease.

Journaling has taught me that I can not be all things to all people, and I am not expected to. It has taught me that I have the right to continue to laugh, to live and to embrace life in as many ways as I can. It has taught me that most of the time I am alone in this darkness and in the sadness of this loss. It has taught me to appreciate simple moments, golden nuggets I call them, and store them away in my heart forever to remember.

This book can't take away the sadness of the disease. Nor can it bring back memory to your loved one or make your life "normal" again. But it can allow you to walk out of your life and into mine where you will find ideas that may help you to come to realize **what** you are feeling, **how** you are feeling and **why** you are feeling is not isolated only to your life.

"A Stranger in the House" is a journal of my reflections, my frustrations and my truths as I know them to be. It was written from the heart, learned from the mind and driven by the spirit.

I am the type of person that always reads the last chapter of a book first. Don't ask me why. I just always need to know how something ends before it begins. And so, as I began to write this book I realized that I had to begin with the ending. The last chapter had to be the first chapter.

Chapter I

"The Last Chapter

I sat holding Ron's hand knowing he would die within five minutes. His breathing was almost 50 seconds apart now. I sat and waited. Another breath. Was this the last one? Holding his hand I said,

"It's just too hard, isn't it Ron? You want to go, don't you? It's okay Honey you can go. I'll be okay, I promise. I love you, I will always love you—now and forever".

He drew his last breath. It was quiet and peaceful. There was no movement, not even a twitch. It was over. From my hands into the hands of God his Spirit flew. He was safe and whole again and for that I was happy.

Chapter II

A Stranger In The House
1999—2001

I opened the envelope from the bank. It was a late notice that we had not paid the monthly car payment. Ron," I yelled, "you forgot to pay the car payment this month."

"Sorry" he said "I thought I did."

"Well, sorry doesn't cut it," I snapped. "Now we have to pay a $20 late fee."

"I'm sorry" he replied, "Didn't you ever forget something."

Of course I had, but I was mad that he didn't remember. After all he was retired—he certainly didn't have that many things on his mind . . .

When Ron retired in 1994, he took over most of the house duties including making dinner every night. After dinner one night, while I was washing the dishes, I happened to notice that he hadn't turned the oven off.

"You left the oven on" I said.

"Sorry" he said,"I guess I forgot."

"Seems like you are forgetting all the time" I replied sarcastically.

"Well I was busy getting everything on the table and just forgot." Seemed logical to me even though I thought it unusual.

"Jacci, do you remember if I took my pills today?" Ron asked. "I can't remember if I took them or not." Ron, who was diabetic and had high blood pressure took medications for both. Pills in the morning and at night. I never kept track of what he took—we were both adults. He was responsible for his personal things and I was responsible for mine. So, every once in a while when he would ask if I remembered whether or not he took his pills I would get irritated.

"Geez Ron, you're retired—you have no responsibilities but to get up in the morning and take your pills and you can't even remember that." But again, he would ask only rarely so it was not "an issue" I became concerned with. Obviously, the only times he was not sure if he had taken his pills was when he said something about it. Or was it? But it did occur enough times I finally went and bought a weekly pill organizer, where he could put his pills in little compartments for each day—morning and night. This appeared to resolve the problem totally.

I can't count the number of times Ron lost his keys, misplaced his wallet or forgot where he had put a tool he wanted to use.

There were so many times that I just felt "something was different" but couldn't yet pin point it. There were days when I came home from work and felt he hadn't moved from his chair the entire day. But whenever I asked how his day was or what he had done—he always had a list a mile long to tell me.

Then there were the phone messages I never received. Weeks later I'd run into someone who mentioned they had called and left a message with Ron for me to call them, but he never told me. I would get upset over it but never attributed it to more than growing older and perhaps being lazy.

I was 28 and Ron was 45 when we were married June 5th, 1977. We had known each other only 3 months when he proposed. I was head over heels in love with him. We were as different as day and night and yet so right for each other. Opposites do attract!

Anyone who knew him knew that he had the ability to talk to anyone—anyplace—anywhere. I would often say he was the only person I knew who could sell snow to Eskimos. After he retired he kept himself busy all the time. Because of our age difference, I was still working fulltime and encouraged him to travel and visit relatives across the country. Every year he would volunteer two weeks in the hills of Kentucky for Habitat. He loved it and they loved him. Life was great and only getting better. In only a few years I would be retiring and our lives would be carefree and fun. We both had looked forward to the day when we could travel and enjoy being able to do all those things in life that you spend the first 55 years of your life simply dreaming about. The kids were grown and on their own. Now was going to be the beginning of the rest of our life together. Isn't this what we work and save for our entire lives? So many plans—so many dreams—never to be realized.

Chapter III

January 17th, 2001
The Day That Changed Our Lives

Ron was scheduled for partial knee replacement. It was a simple routine surgery that would have him up and around within a week. I planned on taking two days off from work—that's all I would need. The surgery went fine, but he had a reaction to the anesthetic which threw him into a full fledged level of Dementia. Had I known the reality of what had been slowly happening the previous two years, another type of anesthetic would have been used. But no one had an inkling that Ron was in the early stages of Alzheimer's.

After surgery Ron had no short term memory. He was very much "in the moment' but as soon as the moment left so did the memory of it. After an MRI, CT, EEG, blood work and testing for Dementia, it was determined Ron was in early stages Alzheimer's. Actually the only way Alzheimer's can be diagnosed is after one dies through an autopsy—but through all these tests everything else can be eliminated. The only thing left is the diagnosis of Alzheimer's. These tests and diagnosis did not happen overnight. It wasn't until eight months later that his Neurologist put him on a medication called Aricept—a drug used for Alzheimer's patients. It doesn't restore your memory, but can significantly slow the progress down. Studies indicate that it will take a person on this medication three years to reach the same level of progression as a person who is not taking it reaches in six months. This is significant, and can prolong quality of life for a substantial long period of time.

I ended up being off work three weeks with Ron after his surgery. It was a scary time for me. So much had changed so quickly, and

I couldn't grasp what was happening, why it was happening and what we could do about it. People would call and as soon as Ron hung up the memory of talking with the person was gone. Friends would come to visit him, and once they walked out the door so was the memory of their being here. I would fix him breakfast and 20 minutes later he would ask what we were going to have for breakfast.

Ron then went through an "I can't" stage. *I can't walk up stairs I can't put on my socks I can't sit on the toilet I can't get into bed.* Actually there wasn't anything he thought he could do. Every moment was a struggle. And because I didn't understand Alzheimer's, know anything about Alzheimer's, nor want to know anything about Alzheimer's, I went into complete denial myself. Something was seriously wrong, and I wasn't going to allow it to be Alzheimer's. I would make Ron overcome this and return to the person I knew. Other people got this disease I told myself. Other people became caregivers to someone they loved— but not me and not Ron. So, I would argue with him, fight with him and insist on his doing and being what he did not want and could not be. This just couldn't be happening to us.

I had to learn to take one day at a time, to deal with what my life was only today. To begin to try and decide on issues that may or may not happen months or years from now was too overwhelming and took away from what I had to accept at that moment.

Tonight, I remember always thinking how truly blessed I have been because even though my mom died in her early 60's and my dad in his 70's, neither had suffered any type of dementia and I never had to deal with this kind of "loss." At my age I have watched friends deal with Alzheimer's with their parents and I thought how terrible to have to live to see your parents change before your eyes and not be able to do anything about it. NEVER did I think there was the most remote possibility of my having to live through this type of disease with Ron, who was always so much "in the now" and his memory sharp as a tack. Never could this happen to us—to him—to me.

Ron had always been overweight and wrestled with high blood pressure and diabetes. For years Doctor Johnson warned him that if he didn't change his life style he would pay dearly for it later in life—but Ron's theory was as long as there was a pill for the ailment he would survive.

People often ask how they will know if they are "getting Alzheimer's." I think the best answer is: *If you remember that you forgot something than you don't have Alzheimer's.* Alzheimer's is forgetting that it happened, and not ever remembering that it ever happened. I can misplace my keys or walk out of the house and forget my purse—but I remember that I did that. Ron does the same thing, but never remembers that he has done it. And because they don't remember that they forgot, they don't know they have a problem.

For the first three months we saw doctors every week. I had specific questions I asked Ron every week and I had to monitor his answers. What Day Is It? What Month Is It? What Year Is It? Who Is The President of the United States? Spell the word "world"—spell it backwards; What are the months of the year? How many children do you have? What are their names? What are their ages? Where do they live? Ron answered these pretty well—but as the weeks progressed the answers changed slightly.

"I notice that Ron's pill organizer is empty and realize he is not taking his daily medications. How many days have gone without him taking his pills? I never had to monitor his meds before. I vow I will not start now—After all he has to get back to doing these things again. I will not succumb to this memory loss. I won't admit this is Dementia or Alzheimer's. Ron had a reaction to his anesthetic and everything I have researched on the internet indicates that his memory could come back in full but it may take up to six months. I need to give this time. Just be patient."

I started making sure Ron's pill bottles were out on the counter for him to fill each week. That way I knew he was taking his pills but he would actually be doing it. Surely he could remember that when the pill box is empty he has to go and fill it again. This will work I told myself.

A week later the pill organizer was empty. I checked it on the last day so I knew he hadn't gone a day without his meds. I asked him why he hadn't filled his pill organizer.

"What pill organizer?" "What pills?" he asked.

This isn't good I thought. I got the bottles of pills and made him fill his weekly organizer. Only next week it was the same thing. The pill box was empty. This time on a gut feeling after he filled it I checked to make sure he hadn't forgotten any pills. The doctor increased his meds significantly in the past months—and he was taking eight pills in the morning and five at night. "Oh My God," he has all different pills in every compartment. What a mess . . . . Is this the way he has been taking them? I can't believe it.

I told him "You put all the wrong pills in the wrong times and days."

He became upset "I don't care," he said.

This has turned into another one of those "I can't" things—"I can't do this." Today was yet another image of "A Stranger in the House".

"I will fill his pill organizer weekly and I will make sure he takes his pills every day. I can do this because this is only temporary. In a few months he'll get his memory back and be "normal" again. This is only temporary . . . ."

"Ron asks the same thing over and over again. We went to the doctor today and he asked me seven times this morning why he had to get up—and where we were going. I am so impatient and keep telling Ron that he repeats himself over and over and I don't want to hear him say it again."

My brother in law, Guy, sent me an email explaining Alzheimer's. I didn't know why he sent it. Ron didn't have Alzheimer's. The article said to teach yourself to hear whatever the person says, how ever many times they say it as "this is the first time I am ever hearing this." Remember, if he remembered saying it he wouldn't be repeating it. In his mind he has never said it before. I finally am beginning to understand. He got agitated at me for yelling at him because he didn't remember repeating himself. This was complicated. The doctor suggested I join a support group for Alzheimer's. I didn't think I needed one. In my journal I write again:

"This is temporary—in six months our lives will be back to "normal." But I will do more research on Dementia to help me through the next few months."

"Every morning is a nightmare. Ron refuses to get up and shower. I am getting up at 5:00 am to get ready for work. It takes me over an hour to get Ron up, showered, dressed and fed before I leave. Honestly, he acts like a kid. He fights about getting into the shower. I think he would go days without a shower. This from a man that showered once and sometimes twice a day. Like a child he dilly dallies around and wastes time. I am exhausted before I get to work. This isn't normal—what is happening?— maybe I should go to a support group meeting. But if I do I'm succumbing to this and I won't. I can deal with this—I am a strong person . . . . In six months things will be better . . .

It was now June and nothing had improved. In fact things were worse. I was worn out. Emotionally, physically, mentally and spiritually. I needed help. I needed answers. I decided to call the Alzheimer's Association.

"I made the call today—the people there were wonderful. The first time in months I talked to someone who honestly knew what I was saying. They gave me the date and time of a support group. I am going. I can't do this alone."

I found the support group to be my reality check. I realized I was dealing with a real disease—a permanent life changing disease and my world was never going to be "normal" again. A woman sobbed because her father refused to shower. "Oh my God—it isn't just me—it isn't just Ron. Everything I'm doing is wrong."

I enrolled Ron in the Safe Return Program through the Alzheimer's Association, an excellent program available to individuals diagnosed with dementia. The concept is simply having the person registered in a computer data base in the event they wander and get lost. They wear a necklace or bracelet with their first name and an ID number which when entered into the computer can locate where they live and the person to contact who is responsible for them. This program also offers the caregiver a bracelet engraved "I am a caregiver for (person's name and ID Number) in the event you are in an accident, someone can be contacted to take care of the Alzheimer's patient. I strongly support this program and would hope all caregivers take advantage of its services.

One week Ron's mom came for a visit. She told me that during the day, while I was at work, Ron would call out for me from his chair. When there was no answer he would panic knowing he is alone and not knowing where I was. Obviously I was not aware of this. There was an easy solution. I took two clipboards and made daily sheets on the computer. The heading read "Today is . . . ." and I wrote in the day and date. At the top of the page I printed some type of picture that would relate what the month was for Ron. For example in October I decorated the top of the page with pumpkins and witches. He then knew what time of year it was also. Next I made a heading "Where Jacci Is" and wrote in where I was and when I would return. The last heading was "People who called on the telephone" and left space for him to write down messages. Placing one of these clipboards at the two places he sat relieved his anxiousness when he called and I didn't answer. I also have no doubt there were many times when he would wonder what month or time of year it was and this was a way of letting him know without him having to get anxious about it.

Then I found an "on line" support room for caregivers to Alzheimer's "victims." Little did I know that these folks were to become my extended family. It would be through them and with them that I would find the answers, the hope, the strength and the courage to walk each step on this journey. Barbara, Nancy, Lou, Felix, Sue, Nan and so many others became my 3:00 am shoulders to cry on, my confidants and my answers to the hundreds of questions that were waiting for me to ask. For the next two years we would become faceless family with hearts ever intertwined together.

"Ninety five percent of the time Ron knows who I am. There are only moments when I appear to be a stranger in his life. And yet, for me, ninety five percent of the time I look at Ron and wonder who this man is. He speaks differently, he thinks differently, he acts differently. I do not know this man. I do not like this man. He is becoming a "Stranger in the House".

Chapter IV

"Making the Pieces Fit"

I believe that God has a purpose and a plan for each of us. That everything in our lives happens for a reason. Most often, I cannot begin to understand the purpose of things that are happening to me, but eventually the pieces come together and the puzzle is complete.

It was on a cold wintry day in the year 2001, that "Mr. Alzheimer's" appeared at our door step and took up residence within Ron's body.

"He" showed up in our lives unexpectedly, without warning or permission. He wanted me to hate him, fight him and give in to him. He wanted to be rid of me so that he could do as he chose as he grew and lived within Ron, controlling all thoughts, words and actions—with only one goal—to destroy his life.

I was scared and angry, but determined not to allow "him" to destroy Ron's life or mine.

When Ron was diagnosed with Alzheimer's I accepted the role of caregiver willingly. I knew little of what it would entail. When people would tell me what a long road I had ahead I was baffled. What did they mean? Certainly it could not be that hard. The pieces of the puzzle were on the table and I was only beginning to put them together.

My faith has always been my lifeline. I had been brought up Protestant, but converted to Catholicism ten years after Ron and I were married. Ron was Catholic and it was after I converted that I realized how much he had missed the faith he had been brought up with.

I know now that God was preparing us years ahead for the journey that awaited us now. I knew God hadn't given this disease to Ron. While I didn't expect a miracle of physical healing for Ron, I did expect that God would walk with us on this journey and it would be with Him, through Him and by Him that only positive would come through for Ron and I.

It was as though Satan had come into our lives as "Mr Alzheimer's" wanting us to give in to him and give up on God.

I'm a firm believer that God can't prevent evil in the world, but He can be there with us through evil, guiding us, and helping us to understand, forgive and accept.

I had no idea what we could learn from this journey. I had no idea what good would come from it. But I knew I had to trust God because without Him I would be alone, scared, and angry.

Some pieces of a puzzle are easy to find; some are difficult. We must not try and make pieces fit that aren't suppose to. We should not try and finish the puzzle too quickly. We need to take our time and allow ourselves to appreciate every piece we find. We must not be afraid to ask others to help us with the pieces and not be afraid to talk about the puzzle with our loved one.

We all have puzzles in life. Usually we are consumed with anxiety, fear and doubt when we are confronted by one. God will give you the pieces for your puzzle. But only you can choose to keep them hidden in the box unopened or empty the box and put the puzzle together one piece at a time. I chose to open the box and put the pieces together. It was not an easy puzzle—but looking back—it was a puzzle Ron and I completed together. It was God's final gift for Ron and I to share together.

Chapter V

Summer 2001

Summer began with Ron and I escaping for five days to an RV Park in our motor home. Best friends Anne and Frank Musto took special care of Ron and I throughout these last years. Frank was there to fix repairs, mow the lawn and get a grip on all the "house stuff" I had never had to do. Anne listened with a caring heart, letting me cry and laugh for as long as I needed.

Everyone should have two such special people in their lives. Frank set up our motor home on their extra lot at Leisurewood Recreational Community in Akron, New York, a small community located outside of Buffalo.

They did everything needed to enjoy it. All we did was show up and relax. This certainly was "camping" at its best.

"Ron does nothing but sit. At least he is outside and getting fresh air. I bought him a pair of gray shorts and matching gray sleeveless top. Every day he insists on wearing this same outfit. He has a zillion outfits but only wants to wear one. I am washing them every day."

I went to my friends on the internet and shared my frustrations. Quickly a response came back "By choosing the same outfit Ron doesn't have to put himself in a position to have to make a decision on what to wear, will it match, is it the right thing to wear. He is afraid of making a mistake and he knows the gray outfit is okay. He won't ask for help or admit he even has a memory problem because he is afraid of his future. At this stage he is simply trying to hide this from you. The answer is simple—go and buy three more sets of the exact same outfit." I was amazed. Every day he put on a "different" set but didn't realize it. He thought he was putting on the same ones. By buying three of the same, I was not washing the same ones every day. It was an eye opener for me. There are always new ways to decrease the stress.

"We returned home from the motor home today to find that our bathroom pipes burst upstairs and our entire upstairs, dining room and spare bedroom downstairs were flooded."

The remainder of the summer was spent dealing with contractors and insurance representatives repairing and remodeling over $25,000 in damages. The saddest part was watching Ron through this process. Ron had owned his own construction company for thirty years and had spent the last twelve years working as a Construction Superintendent for New York State. His life was building and he had the reputation of always believing there wasn't a project he couldn't do quicker, better or cheaper than the next guy. But now, it was different. Ron didn't have any interest at all in the repair or remodeling of the house. He sat day after day in his chair while the men were here working, as though he didn't know the difference between a hammer and a screw driver. It was during these months that the reality of this disease flowed through my veins. This was not Ron. This was not the man I married. A new identity was emerging within him. Yes, indeed, there was A Stranger in the House.

As the summer days continued it seemed as though each week brought a new awareness into my life. Sometimes I didn't think I could keep up with the quickness of the changes. Changes that were small but defining. Having never been a care giver and never involved with this illness, my life had turned into a crisis and the one person that was always there to help me through was no longer there for me.

"I left Ron notes every day this week to mow the lawn and he hasn't. Today I called him to remind him to mow. I came home to find he had only mowed the center part of the lawn. When I asked why, he said he thought he had mowed it all. The next three

days found me coming home to find he had removed the same part of the lawn each day. The grass is five times higher around the house than where he is mowing. How can he not know where he should mow? None of this makes sense to me. Twice this month we have been traveling in the car and Ron has lost control of his bowels. He has no warning. One more thing I guess I will need to begin to monitor."

Alzheimer's patients develop silly things they will insist on doing. At first you find yourself fighting with them not to do them, as they are silly and make no sense. You will find yourself getting angry, losing patience and becoming stressed by their repeated behavior. Everyone is different. Some people put on goofy clothes, while some carry something odd with them all the time.

With Ron, he has this obsession that he HAS to have a pillow between his knee and the car door when he is in the car or he is "in pain". You must learn to just accept these insignificant incidences. The truth is they are not hurting anyone and it brings them comfort and peace. It calms them so let them do it. A lady in my support group tells how she fought with her mother for weeks because her mother insisted on wearing a knit hat while watching Television. She would make her take it off and her mom would become aggressive, agitated and angry. Finally she just said, "Fine! Wear the damn hat". Her mom would sit for hours laughing and watching television, happy and secure.

Is this normal? Perhaps it's not what normal once was. But there is a new normality in our life, and this is part of it. What is normal now is hearing the same conversation twenty times and listening to it every time as if it were the first. Normal is allowing ourselves to be the person our loved one sees us to be at that moment. Normal is appreciating the simple moments of holding his hand, hearing his laugh, watching him sleep. And what is "normal" in my life today will change as time goes on.

"Tonight was special. Ron and I went with a group of friends on the "Miss Niagara" Boat. It was a three hour ride down the

Niagara River. A beautiful night, warm with just a slight breeze. As Ron and I were standing on deck enjoying the scenery, I felt Ron's arm tightly around my waist. At that moment he was very much "with me" and it felt "normal." I wanted to freeze that moment in time, that feeling, because I knew this was simply the exception and may never happen again. I stared at his face, I placed my head on his shoulder and we stood with our arms around each other for the entire ride. For a short three hours God gave me back "My Ron" and I knew I would forever remember this night together."

Chapter VI

SEPTEMBER 11TH, 2001

Twenty-four hours a day Ron would have the television on. He would sleep, eat and stare into space but the Television had to be on. Today would be no different.

I, like every other American, can tell you exactly where I was and what I was doing when I heard the news about the planes crashing into the World Trade Center.

I was at my desk at work, doing morning daily reports, when a customer came into the office and announced that an airplane had crashed into the World Trade Center. I, like everyone else, thought it was an awful "accident" obviously it could not have been intentional. A few minutes later a co-worker who had logged unto the internet yelled out

"Oh My God! Another plane has hit the Twin Towers."

We all looked at each other in disbelief. Two accidents? What's happening? It couldn't have been intentional. What's happening? What in God's name is happening?

Working for a Government Agency, within minutes we were advised we were on "high alert" status. For the next three hours we were glued to the radio and television, along with all of America. When we realized that

"something" was terribly wrong, live on television, I knew I had to call Ron and find out how he was dealing with all of this.

When I called he told me that he had the television on, "Buildings are on fire" he said. "Planes are crashing into buildings and I am scared."

I told him "I'll be home soon" and I said "don't worry."

Our Agency closed at noon. We were told to go home to be with our family and children. When I arrived home I found Ron staring at the television in disbelief.

By now the Twin Towers had crumbled and they were replaying the images of the planes hitting the Twin Towers and the buildings on fire over and over again. The problem was that Ron didn't realize they were replaying it and kept seeing it as if it were happening "now."

"These buildings keep burning and planes keep crashing into buildings and buildings keep falling down," he said. "They can't stop them, they keep falling"

I finally had to find a cable station that didn't have this news on it for him to watch. Fortunately within a few minutes he had forgotten all about 9/11 and would never think about it again.

It was reported on the news the next day that nursing homes for dementia patients had this same problem and had to literally turn the television off as these patients could not grasp what was happening.

For the next two years Ron would never remember the events of 9/11. A day that changed the world, a day that changed America's sense of security forever, would never enter into Ron's life again. For the first time

I saw a positive side of Alzheimer's. Ron's world would remain safe and secure.

Chapter VII

FALL—2001

You want to believe that everyone is sympathetic to this illness. Certainly no one would intentionally take advantage of someone in this situation. But sadly there are, and it is up to us, as care givers, to become our loved ones eyes, ears and mind. This was a hard lesson for me to learn. We had signed up for a satellite dish the previous year. The past three months Ron had not been able to remember how to work the remote to select or scan the channels. It was just too complicated for him to remember. On the last day of our contract I called the company but because the account was in Ron's name, only he could cancel it.

I explained Ron's condition, put him on the telephone and had him say to the representative "This is Ronald Reed and I want to cancel my contract."

I could tell more was being said and Ron looking confused finally saying "I'm not sure if I should or not."

I took the phone and asked the man what he was telling Ron. He rudely and abruptly told me it was none of my business and he wasn't going to talk to me. After I insisted, he said he was offering my husband "other options" so he wouldn't cancel his contract.

I was furious. How dare he take advantage of a person who he knew had Alzheimer's, and could not or would not remember what he was doing. I made sure he understood this conduct would not be tolerated and I was going to report him and his company to the Attorney General's Office as well as write a letter to his main office. But through this, I learned an important lesson. From now on I would always look out for Ron. For so many years he was my protector and my security. Now I had to learn how to be his.

It was September, and Ron's son, Rob, was getting married in Rochester, NY, about an hours ride from Buffalo. We went for the weekend. It was the first time we had been away since all this began,

"Are we here for one of the grandchildren's baptisms" Ron asked in the hotel room. One more sign of the progress of his memory loss. The day of the wedding, he was very much "in the moment'—He enjoyed the day

He seemed to know everyone and had a great time. The next day we came home and his best friend, Don, called him on the phone.

"Where were you" Don asked. "Oh, we went to Rochester for my granddaughters birthday" Ron said. And so it goes . . . .

October was beautiful, but then fall always is in New York. The leaves paint the streets an array of colors that glisten as the sun shines on them. I love fall, it is my favorite season of the year. Sometimes there are humorous moments such as the entry I wrote in my journal that read:

"Today was a little chilly. I took Ron for a ride to enjoy the foliage. For three hours Ron repeatedly said "Gee, it's getting chilly outside, pretty soon I will have to get my warmer jacket out." He said this over and over again, not once or twice but at least a hundred times. I thought I would scream hearing it one more time. I pretended each time it was the first time he had said it, trying hard to accept and understand. As we were walking into the house Ron says one more time "Gee it's getting chilly outside, pretty soon I will have to get my warmer jacket out." I was ready to blow! So I turned to him and said quite sarcastically; "Gee Ron, it's getting chilly outside, pretty soon you will have to get your warmer jacket out". Without missing a beat he looked at me and said "Oh, I don't know. We still have a few warm days left before I need to get my jacket out." Welcome to the world of Alzheimers!"

"Tonight Ron is just sitting and staring into no where and I think how sad his life has become. And at the same time I think how

blessed I am to have had him in my life. There are times when I think how hard it is for him, and for me, and wonder if it's fair for him to have to continue living like this. I thought as I looked at him tonight that I am so glad I still have him with me. I can still make him laugh, I can still hear his voice, I can still smell his aftershave. There will come a day when I won't have any of those things and I will only be able to remember what I have today. So I need to appreciate it, embrace it and enjoy it. I need to hold on to what I have today and give thanks for it."

It was December and things seemed to be leveling off. We did the "20 questions" every week to calculate his progress. Ron was pretty much living in the 50's and 60's. Those are the years he remembered without flaw. He felt comfortable talking about those times because he remembered them so well. If you asked him who the President was he'd tell you "Johnson". Asking him what the day, date or year was would get you an answer, "I don't know and I don't care." He would try and bluff the doctors with his answers. When the doctor asked him "what did you have for breakfast this morning?" he quickly answered, "Same thing I had yesterday morning."

The most obvious change these past three months was his personality. Ron was always the person that could walk into a room full of strangers and ten minutes later everyone would know him. He could talk about anything to anyone. Now his personality is what I call "flat." He really didn't have one. He tried to stir the conversation to times in his life he could remember but when conversations occurred on present issues he never spoke a word. This was explained by the fact that the person finally realizes they really do have a problem but doesn't want to admit it. They don't want to be

"caught" forgetting or letting others see them as they are, so they begin to withdraw, wanting to stay by themselves. They tend not to want to go out and when they do, they want to go back home immediately. "Home" becomes their safety net, their comfort zone, their security.

I knew Christmas would be difficult. We would celebrate with his children and grandchildren the Saturday before Christmas, and on Christmas day it would be just the two of us. Ron always said I was like "a little kid who loved presents" and every year he'd wait until after I went to bed on Christmas Eve, then put my gifts under the tree. It was like this for 24 years. This year, however, I knew would be different. I told myself a thousand times that he wouldn't remember to buy me a gift and although more than once I thought of buying some gifts, wrapping them, and putting them under the tree for me from him—I never did. I knew it would be okay—there would still be Midnight Mass—we would still be able to do traditional things.

Christmas Eve found Buffalo, New York buried in seven feet of snow. There was no way getting to Midnight Mass. I went to bed early totally confident I was in control of my emotions. I woke up at 4:00 am and saw "lights on". I went to the family room and saw the tree lights on and the tree absolutely bare underneath it. I can't explain the reality of my heart at that moment.

I went down and sat by the tree with the fireplace on and just sobbed. *This was reality. This was truth. I had lost Ron. I was living with a stranger in my house.*

I looked up and Ron was standing next to me asking, "why are you crying? What is wrong?"

The more I said "nothing" the more he asked.

"It's Christmas, Ron—It's Christmas day Ron" I finally said.

He looked at me and than at the tree and just said "Oh my God, I forgot Christmas, I didn't remember to buy you a gift." And he started sobbing.

For the next hour we held each other and just cried. He kept hitting his head and saying "I hate this head thing—I hate this head thing—I just want to die." I held him until he went to sleep. By the time he woke up I was in control and had put all things in perspective. I realized that I had prepared my mind—but not my heart and that I needed to prepare all of me during these times. When he woke up he didn't remember any of it. The day went on without him knowing it was Christmas.

Chapter VIII

Winter—2002

There are things you learn about Alzheimer patients that might help you as their caregiver. For example did you know that for some reason they do not look higher than their head. This comes in handy if you need to hide things from them. Ron is fairly tall—over 6 feet—but I would still put things high up and he never looked there. When I told my doctor this he disregarded it and said he never heard of it—but caregivers all experience the same thing and as far as I am concerned, it is true!

I remember at my first support group meeting being told the importance of taking charge of our finances, reviewing our Wills and Insurance Policies and deciding whether we should continue to live in our house. It was a new year and I knew I had to begin to address these issues. I had put all of this off because I continued to believe, or at minimum wanted to believe, that Ron would magically wake up one morning and our lives would return to "normal". I can look back over the past year and in a strange way Ron and I were both going through the early stages of Alzheimers. I was in the early stages of learning, understanding and accepting and Ron in early stages of the disease itself. I have spent months dealing with emotions, now there were important issues I needed to act on. My first issue was our Wills, Health Proxy and Power of Attorney. This was difficult for me to do as it was one more step on this journey. I felt as though I was giving in—giving up to Alzheimer's. But the reality was I needed to know Ron would be taken care of if something happened to me and things were in place so his children could do what needed to get him the care he would need.

"We went to the Attorney today. I had spoken to him over the phone and told him what I needed. I explained Ron's situation. He suggested that I change my Will so that my step son is Executor. Also I now have Power of Attorney over all of Ron's affairs—this will prevent another episode that occurred with that Satellite TV Company from ever happening again. I can now legally speak on his behalf—I also had my step son given Power of Attorney in the event that I should become unable to care for Ron. Our Health Proxies are in place. Today was "grow up time" a moment of reality—of sadness—of relief . . . ."

I began thinking of selling the house and moving into a free maintenance apartment. I sat Ron down and asked how he would like to live in a smaller place. He was livid. It was more than anger. I could see in his face this emotion of fear. I realized then to uproot him from the one place he felt secure and safe to a new environment would be the worse thing for me to do. He still remembered every square foot of this house. He did little but sit in his chair and watch TV but it was his comfort zone and he was calm and peaceful. There could come a day, all too soon, when he may need to be in long term care. So I was now looking at keeping the house—making it handicapped accessible for him so I knew he would be safe—and when he needed to be moved he would only have to move once.

One day Ron called me at work and said he had a terrible stomach ache. When I got home and made dinner he hardly ate. He said he was really sick. He felt lousy all night. I asked if he had eaten lunch and he said no—so I assumed he must be getting the flu.

The next morning when I took the garbage out on the porch, I saw all my valentine boxes spread over the table. I had bought chocolate valentine hearts for my seven grandchildren with their names on them for Valentines Day. Every box I picked up was empty. Ron had eaten all the candy. I went into the bedroom and asked if he had eaten all the candy the day before. Of course he didn't remember. No wonder he had a stomach ache. Seven chocolate hearts at six ounces a heart—over two pounds of candy!!! And Ron is diabetic.

To see the lighter side of life—he actually ate every chocolate heart but the one that had his name on it. Go Figure . . . .

"We went shopping today and I let Ron drive—it has been a while since I have been with him while he drove and I wanted to see how he was doing. For months now I have known the issue of giving up his license was going to have to be dealt with. But even the mention of the word and Ron would get furious. Giving up your license is like giving up your life. He did fine driving to the store but he asked me eight times on the way "where are we going first". The first time I didn't catch on and just answered him. The second time I thought "what does he mean "first"? This store was the only place we were going. Than I realized it was his way of trying to find out where he was supposed to go without asking or admitting he did not know. I knew than he was not safe to drive alone."

The next day I made up a letterhead for the Department of Motor Vehicles. I wrote a letter to Ron using this creative letterhead telling him that they had been advised by his doctor he had been diagnosed with

Dementia and effective immediately his license would be revised to read that he could only drive with another licensed driver in the car. I also put in the letter this restriction would be reassessed in six months. Now mind you this letter had no date on it—wasn't signed and didn't state his doctor's name. He never questioned the authenticity of the letter. He was madder than a wet hen when he got it. But after two days, he never mentioned it again. I took his truck key off his key ring but he never knew it. He still carried his keys in his pockets and it made him feel as though he was still driving. When he asked about driving, I would show him the letter and tell him he had to wait six months. He didn't like it but he didn't drive. Without a time frame and without a date on the letter—six months would last forever.

Ron no longer had any concept of time. It has been a year now and the diagnosis was over. There is no treatment, and we're just taking one day at a time. Ron sits and sleeps most of the time. He is still very much in the moment, but once the moment is over it is over.

I bought Ron's children the book "The 36 Hour Day" which is on Alzheimer's and the path most patients follow. It's a pretty intense book but very well written. It has been difficult for his children to understand this disease and what the future will hold. I encouraged them to call and visit, but living out of town doesn't make it easy. This could be a time for them to resolve old issues and develop a new relationship with their father. Ron would ask if his children had called and I told him "yes", that they called every week even if they didn't. You learn to take advantage of the memory loss. He didn't remember if his children called or not, and it made him feel "happy" if I told him they had.

Chapter IX

Who is Ron Reed?

As any caregiver will tell you, the one thing you seem to do more and more is reminisce about the past. Perhaps it's because we have more "idle" time at home. Perhaps the reality of life and death is staring us right in the eye. Perhaps it's because we don't want to let go of what we had. When life is "normal" we seldom take time to sit and reflect on the past. We are too busy living in the present and making plans for the future. As a caregiver, we hate living in the present and can't begin to look into the future, so I suppose all we have is the past to "live for".

Ron was born on May 26, 1932. A "Gemini" in the truest sense of the word. Gemini means twins and there were two personalities in Ron. One I fell in love with, the other I tolerated. One was egotistical, stubborn and argumentative. The other was quiet, passionate and caring. The best side of him was reserved to be shared with only a handful of people. How unfortunate so few knew the Ron behind the mask of that Gemini Twin.

He was born the oldest of five siblings; Donna, Jim, Patrick, Guy and Kelly. He joined the Navy in 1949 and served during the Korean War. He loved telling stories of his tour of duty in French Morocco. He married Agnes Keehler in 1953 and they had four children; David, Mary Catherine (who died at birth), Colleen and Robert. For reasons that have nothing to do with this book they divorced but remained good friends throughout their lives.

When Ron and I met in 1976 he was 43, I was 27. He knocked me off my feet. At over 6 feet tall, handsome and charming he was pathetically irresistible. He had a smile that you couldn't say no to.

When he hugged you, your world became safe and secure. You knew he would always protect you.

Ron was a charmer and definitely a "ladies man." I'm not sure if it was his voice, his eyes or just plain old Charisma. But women, young and old alike, stuck to him like fleas on a dog. As he approached life into his 60's I found this to be truer with older widows.

One year after Ron retired I gave him a membership to the athletic club in our area. They had a pool there and I knew he would enjoy being able to go there and swim. He decided he wanted to join their water aerobics class. When he got home the first day he called me at work.

"I was the only man there" he said. "And the local TV station was there doing a story on the aerobics water class and there I was the only man with four women". That night on the local television news was Ron—in the water with the four women.

"Well" I said, "I can guarantee you that the next time you go those four women will have multiplied into twice as many."

"What do you mean" he said.

"Ron, to those ladies you are "live bait" and they will be there to see which one can catch you," He laughed and said I was crazy.

The next week when he went he came home laughing. "You were right! Today there were six new ladies—all widows and ready to invite me to coffee, lunch and dinner."

I think it's at this point in my life that I seem to remember every memory Ron and I have shared. Twenty-seven years of memories and I'm living each and everyone over again. How he would hold my hand whenever we walked together. How he always put his arm around me to let me know "he was there." How we never left each other without a kiss and a "I love you", even when we were mad at each other. How we could argue over the silliest things, and how we enjoyed "making up" after.

When we bought our house in 1977, it was a "handy mans dream." Throughout the years, Ron had turned it into a showplace. Our house was his legacy. That's why he was so comfortable here now. That's why he wanted to die in his house. This house was a part of his being.

I could write a book on memories of family, friends and Ron. I will simply say he loved his children, his mother, his friends and family. If Ron loved you, he loved you forever. He was rough and rugged on the outside, but a marshmallow on the inside. Ron Reed was a mixture of being caring, argumentative, stubborn, compassionate, bossy, loving, secure and insecure. A complex guy living a simple life as best he knew how.

I remember all the birthdays, holidays, parties we shared and wondered how all these years went by so quickly. We had done so much, yet in a blink of an eye it seemed that everything happened at once. I could not imagine my life without Ron and yet I knew he was slowly leaving me. What would I do without him? What would my life be like?

Chapter X

Spring 2002

"Ron got up by himself this morning and took a shower—He loves the new handicapped shower we had installed. I hope this continues. I had forgotten how nice it was not to start the day off without a fight over showering. We went to 800 am Mass—I watched Ron during Mass—He knew all the prayers just like he always did. He struggled with sitting and standing and didn't even attempt to kneel. Most of the afternoon he just sat in his chair. Tonight he called for me to come and help him out of his chair. This has been happening a lot lately—He says he can't get out of the chair. He has a doctor's appointment tomorrow—will ask doctor about it."

The doctor found Ron had gained 12 lbs. He was up to 318. He had never been that heavy. The doctor stressed that Ron had to be more active. He spoke to Ron as if he had no problem with Dementia at all. It made me wonder if doctors realize the extent of dementia. Of course Ron agreed and promised to diet and be more active. After we left the office we stopped for breakfast. He ordered bacon and eggs.

"Remember what the doctor told you," I said. "You have to lose weight!" Reluctantly he changed his order to poached eggs and wheat toast. I went to the restroom, and when the waitress brought our food there was bacon and sausage links on his plate with a side platter of pancakes.

"Why is there bacon and sausage links on your plate? And why are there pancakes?" I asked.

The waitress responded "He changed his order while you were gone".

As soon as I had left the table he ordered more food. This journey was moving forward.

"Today Dorothy, our friend Frank's mom, died. I called Ron to tell him but by the time I got home he had forgotten. These are the times that I miss my Ron the most. He's sad at the moment then its over and that's that. I want to talk, and cry, and remember, but there's no one I can do that with anymore."

"I bought a ham to bake to take to Anne and Franks to help them through the next few days dealing with Dorothy's death. Today Ron called me at work and said he was baking the ham. Oddly, he remembered the ham was for Anne and Frank. Ron loved cooking and he took special pride of his baked hams. Glazed with his special 'mix" and completed with his array of cherries and pineapple, it was always delicious. I was so pleased that he had remembered, that he wanted to do this for our dear friends. When I arrived home I found the ham on the stove covered with foil and ready to deliver. I asked him if he had any problems getting the ham ready. He answered "Not at all" Wanting to see the masterpiece myself, I took the foil off the pan to find the ham sitting there, plain and uncooked. That is all he had done was put the ham in the pan. We took the ham, as it was, to Anne and Frank.

May found me realizing my relationship with Ron had changed. I watch his every move. When we're at a restaurant, I automatically choose a table near the restroom and take the chair facing the door to the restroom. No one else can see the fear in his eyes the second he walks into the room. It's the fear of a child who has lost their parent. When he comes out of the restroom he can immediately see me and not panic as to where he is or where he should go. And when he sees me there is that wonderful, childlike smile again.

The truth is he is no longer my husband. I am no longer his wife—I am his caregiver. Yes indeed, there is A Stranger in the House.

"I didn't sleep last night. I laid awake until 3:00 am just staring at the ceiling. Thinking about everything and looking into the future which I don't usually allow myself to do. Ron was so peaceful sleeping. I kept thinking at least how good it is that he isn't worrying about his future—our future—my future."

"This has been a day that I will remember forever. I wish I could relive this day every day of my life!!! We celebrated Ron's 70th birthday. I planned a big birthday party at a restaurant with our relatives and friends. Ron was in his glory and knew what was happening every moment. By tonight he had already started to forget it. Today was what I call a "Hallmark Moment" for our family and one of those "golden nuggets" I will cherish in my heart forever."

By June, Ron was losing things left and right. First he lost his emerald ring. He lost his wallet so many times I finally took everything out of it but his license and his "Safe Return Card." He insisted he had to have a credit card and cash so I put one of those fake ones you get in the mail and some monopoly money. The "credit card" didn't even have his name on it, but he thought he had a credit card and he was happy. No matter how many times I did these "fake" things it never ceased to amaze me that he never caught on. At this time on the journey I have come to realize that all of these things need to be done as they make his life easier to cope with and my life easier to deal with.

"I have come to the conclusion that Ron has the ability to see through walls. It never fails that when he calls me to bring him something, or when I go back into the other room and my backside only begins to touch the seat of the chair, is when I hear "Honey, can you come here a minute?" God forbid he ever ask

for two things at the same time. It's as if he can see through those walls to know the second I'm about to sit down. The majority of me knows this is not intentional, but there is a tiny part of me that just wonders "if" he isn't enjoying this attention.

Chapter XI

Facts for Caregivers

A National Study shows that 13% of the workforce retire specifically to become a fulltime caregiver for a loved one. Although that percentage is fairly low other statistics prove that one out of every three folks will spend one to four years of their retirement as a fulltime caregiver. And it goes without saying that if you are not a primary caregiver you will become involved in a care giving situation, whether it be short term or long term, sometime within your life.

The American Association of Retired Persons has done extensive surveys on Care Giving in the United States. Their reports show that at the present time a little over 25 % of American households contain a family caregiver. They project that by the year 2020 ten million people, age 50 and over, in this country will need long term care and because of high cost the responsibilities will fall on family members to care for these people at home.

Additionally, their survey shows almost 50% of the present workforce engage in care giving for an older or disabled loved one.

A National Study on Women and Care giving highlighted the conflicting demands of work and elder care. This study shows that working women who are caregivers:

- 33% were forced to decrease their working hours
- 29% passed by job promotions, training opportunities or new assignments
- 22% were required to take an unpaid leave of absence
- 20% were forced to switch from working fulltime to part time

- 16% found they had to quit their jobs to become full time caregivers.
- 14% elected to take early retirement to take on the task of fulltime caregiver

Interestingly, approximately 75% of those providing care to older family members are female.

Also there is a misconception this is an "older person" problem. I found through my research that the average age of a family care giver who is caring for someone aged 50 and over is only 46 years old.

And one additional research study, conducted by the Alzheimer's Association, suggests the unpaid family care giver has saved the American taxpayer over 35 billion dollars in the cost of caring for persons with Alzheimer's alone.

In one long term facility, it was discovered that if they keep everything looking like 50 years ago the patients did so much better. This long term facility is totally decorated in 1950's décor, from furniture to foods to TV programs. The patients are calmer and happier because this is the "time" they are most comfortable in. I could relate all of this to Ron. He loved talking about the 50's and 60's.

There are wonderful seminars and lectures available through the Alzheimers Association and various HMO's. I was notified there would be an informational seminar with Olympia Dukakis as the guest speaker. Her mother had Alzheimers and Mrs. Dukakis does speaking engagements sharing her experiences as she walked this journey with her mother. Before Mrs. Dukakis spoke, there were three Neurologists who spoke on the various stages of Alzheimer's, what to expect, how to accept and care for your loved one and the importance of continuing to care for your own needs. I had taken a seat in the front side row and was mesmerized by all that I was hearing and learning from these professionals. A woman, the only other person sitting in the row, sat two seats down from me. When one of the speakers had finished I turned to her and said "Isn't this interesting?"

She responded "Yes, I only wish I had attended something like this earlier on".

I asked "Do you have a loved one with Alzheimer's"?

She smiled and said "My mother died of Alzheimer's but I knew so little of the disease than".

I said I was sorry to hear it and turned my attention to the person who was now starting to introduce the main speaker, Olympia Dukakis.

As the introduction was being made, the woman next to me stood up and began walking to the stage. I thought, what is she doing? She better sit back down, when I realized "that woman" was Olympia Dukakis! What an honor for me to have spoken to her caregiver to caregiver.

I was amazed at the insight Mrs. Dukakis offered to her audience. She spoke about her fears of having to see her mother see her as someone else—perhaps an aunt or a sister or her grandmother— and how she would learn to cope with her inability to know her. She offered some excellent advice. She said that instead of being uncomfortable with her mother "seeing" her as someone other than who she was, she simply allowed herself to become "that person". If her mother saw her as her mother's sister, she became her mother's sister. She would ask her mother to tell her what her best memory was of her. Her mother would reminisce about a past memory and time, one that Olympia had never known or heard. Olympia said that it was during this period she came to learn so many wonderful memories of her mothers young childhood, and young adulthood that she would never have known.

I thought to myself what a wonderful way to accept this stage of Alzheimer's. Instead of brooding over the fact that her mother didn't know her for herself, she embraced the opportunity to connect deeper and more intimately with her mother than ever before. A wonderful example of deciding whether you want to look at the glass as half empty or half full. I remembered this advice throughout my journey with Ron. By allowing myself to be the person he saw me to be I came to know many wonderful stories and times in Ron's life that I had never known before. Remember, this does not have to be the saddest time in your life.

Mrs Dukakis spoke how important it is to communicate with your loved one, even if you don't believe they are listening or can relate. She shared with us a moment with her mom and her daughter. Olympia and her daughter had gone to visit her mom in her Nursing Home. Olympia's daughter sat on her grandmother's bed and told her about her boyfriend and how she was thinking of breaking up with him because of something he had done. She patted her grandmother's hand and said "Oh grandma, if only you could tell me what to do". As Olympia and her daughter were going to their cars after their visit, her daughter stopped and said she really wanted to go back in and spend a few more minutes with her grandmother. The daughter walked back into her grandmother's room and as she stood at her bed, her grandma opened her eyes, looked right at her, smiled and said "Dump the bastard". The reality is, we never know just how much they really are with us and we always need to believe they are with us.

On one occasion Ron woke me up and asked me what year it was. I told him 2003.

"Holy Cow" he said. "We will be married 50 years this year. You know I remember our very first date."

I knew he was seeing me as his previous wife, Agnes. Curious I let him tell me all about their first date, exactly where he went to pick her up, who they went out with, where they went. He remembered every detail.

Than he said, "You know I knew I would love you the first time I kissed you."

Knowing I was getting myself into possible difficult memories, I finally said, "Ron, you know I think you are remembering Agnes and not me. We have only been married 26 years" "Oh", he said, "that's right". Going out on a limb, I asked him "Do you remember our first date?"

He tried relentlessly to remember but could not. I told him "That's okay, honey, it doesn't matter." With his arm around me hugging me, he smiled and looked at me and said "I may not remember our first date but I know I must have had a good time cause I'm still here."

That was my Ron, always able to come through with a line to make you feel everything was okay.

Chapter XII

The Quality of an Hour

I decided that I had to devote an entire Chapter to this experience. I was afraid if I just put this in the middle of a Chapter it wouldn't be read or understood. If there is anything in this book that is important to remember this Chapter is. This is a story every care giver needs to hear. On March 12th, 2002 I wrote in my journal:

"Tonight I attended my support group meeting. We meet for two hours from 6:00 pm until 8:00 pm. The evening went pretty much as usual. The same frustrations—the same questions— the same fears. It was almost 8:00 pm and the meeting was winding down. Our leader asked if anyone had anything they wanted to add before we left. "Susan" a woman in her 60's raised her hand and just began to cry. 'I feel so angry, so guilty, so resentful and so ashamed. I put my husband into a nursing home two months ago. He seldom remembers who I am, sits and sleeps most of the time. I just couldn't take care of him at home any longer. He is in a good facility and he is getting good care. I go there every day and stay there all day long. It is hard for me to say this but I hate it. I hate going there and just sitting for hours and hours. At least at home I could do things, there I do nothing. He sleeps or stares at me as though I am a stranger. I find myself leaving him with anger in my heart every day. He doesn't even know I am there. I come in and if he does know me he accuses me of not being there for months. People say I should only go every other day but than I would feel guilty. How can I go on with my life knowing he is just existing in his. I am so depressed. I just don't want to live.'

"Our leader hesitated for a moment and than said to the group, "You know our meeting should be ending, but this is such an important issue, can you stay a little longer?"

We all said yes. Our leader began "Putting your loved one into a Nursing Facility will probably be the hardest decision you will have to make. We all want our loved one to have the best care and we all believe that we are the ones that can give them that care. There comes a time when the realization that we cannot physically, mentally and emotionally do what has to be done. Once we accept that and follow through by placing the person into long term care, guilt overwhelms our lives. Whether we had promised our loved one that we would never do this or whether we promised ourselves we would never do this, the guilt of having to "let go" becomes a part of our every moment. And so we believe that we must be with our loved one every hour, every day.

Only now, there isn't anything we really have to do for them and so we find ourselves sitting and staring and waiting. Waiting for the hours to pass so the day will pass so we can go home, and wait until the next day when we can do this all over again.

The thought of not going every day fills us with more guilt than going. Susan, you are not alone in feeling the way you do. But, I want to share with you a study that was done by an Alzheimer's Long Term Care Facility. They monitored their patients and their visitors.

The family member who came everyday and spent hours and hours with their love one, just sitting there, just "being there", and leaving feeling resentful and angry, the staff found that the patient was left irritable, would not eat, sleep and was anxious the rest of the day. But the person who came to visit their loved one and only stayed an hour or so—but in that hour spent their time talking to their loved one, holding their hand, combing their hair, making them laugh, kissing their forehead, after they left the staff found the patient was "happy and content" the entire day. They ate well, slept well, and smiled and responded in a happy way. In both scenarios, when the person left, the patient did not remember they had been there, did not remember what they said or did. 50

The difference was that the short visit was filled with "happy feelings" and those feelings remained within the person after the visit had ended. They didn't know who gave them the happy feelings, they didn't know what the happy feelings were, they just knew they had a happy feeling within them."

Our leader could not stress enough to us, that it is not so important the number of hours we be with the person, it is what we do with the hour that we are with them. And, knowing that we are leaving the person happy and content, we can visit them and leave without feelings of guilt or resentment.

I know I have a long way to go before I have to think about Nursing Home care for Ron. But I also know I will never forget what I experienced tonight. "Susan" left our meeting with a new understanding of how she can be there for her husband and still have a life for herself. It is so easy for us, as caregivers, to think we have to do it all by ourselves. Sometimes we do too much without even knowing it. We can learn to do what needs to be done and we can still enjoy a moment or two of life without guilt or resentment. This is why this support group is so important. We learn from each other and we have a leader that is a professional to guide us and teach us how to get through this darkness. I am so grateful for the Alzheimer's Association Support Group. I will sing this organizations praises for the rest of my life!"

For those who are reading this that are experiencing their loved one in a Long Term Nursing Facility, remember it is the quality of your time, not your quantity. One hour of quality love can fill them with a day of inner happiness. One hour of quality love will give you the peace of mind to leave and live and laugh without guilt or resentment or anger.

Chapter XIII

Summer—2002

I've never walked for any charity in my life. Not because I don't believe in charities, but because walking usually means activity and I would rather write a check than participate. I was compelled to help in any way I could to support the Alzheimer's Association for continued research. I just knew that with the necessary research our children and definitely our grandchildren would never have to worry about this monster of a disease. So. I signed up to walk in the Annual Memory Walk to raise money for research for Alzheimer's. I asked everyone I knew to sponsor me and I raised over $400. I only had to walk three miles but for me it was a marathon!!! But I did it. I did it for Ron. When I got home Ron saw the brochure on Alzheimer's and asked who we knew that had Alzheimer's. When I told him he did, he cried.

He just looked at me and said "I knew I had a memory problem but I thought I would be okay in a week or two."

He had no idea he had been walking this journey for 1 ½ years. In his mind, it had been "a week or two." The one good thing was right after dinner he had forgotten all about our conversation. He was no longer upset. How I wish I could forget about it too—it lives in him but it lives with me. There's a big difference in that.

"I find it harder and harder to journal every day. In the beginning I was looking for new developments with Ron every day, watching his every move and word. It feels as though now I know pretty much what he is going to do and how he is going to act and unless a significant new sign occurs, what use to appear to be "Not Normal" is now "Normal" in my life. I know it is

important to keep track of daily progressions but sometimes I think if I don't write about it than I don't have to deal with it—it "just is". It is simply a roller coaster—one moment he is alert and "knowing" and the next he is passive and "out of it". They say this is what it will be like so I might as well get use to it."

I found Ron was much more alert and active when I was home on weekends. Working fulltime all week limited the amount of time I could be home. I really needed to begin working part time. I had enough vacation time that I could work half days and still be on payroll fulltime. I was so fortunate that he didn't wander or get into things he should not. In my support group there are so many that have to deal with so much more than I.

There are notes taped all over the house. On the stove there is a note that says "Do Not Use—Not Working". A "Do Not Touch" note on the thermostat and a "Do Not Open" note on the fireplace door. A Caregiver's house is filled with notes—notes—notes!!!!

Ron has five doctors caring for him. It seems as though we are at a doctor's office every week. When his prostate doctor came out and told me Ron thought he was there to have his feet examined I knew it was now time for me to go with him into the examining room. Those with Alzheimer's have no patience. Therefore, it's imperative to schedule the very first or very last appointment of the day. Still, it was a no win situation. If I make him the first appointment that involves getting him up early to get ready in time to be there which he hates. If I make the last appointment we end up waiting. If I only could find a doctor who's first appointment was at 11:00 am!!

"It's 3:00 am and I can't sleep. I might as well journal my thoughts. Ron is sleeping like a baby. I suppose it's better than some folks who have Alzheimer's—they don't sleep at all. That would be worse by far. I'm wondering about Ron—what stage he really is in. Am I pushing panic buttons that I shouldn't be? Am I seeing everything that's happening? Am I missing anything ? How long do we have? How long does he have? And my greatest fear is that something will happen to me and I don't know who

will care for him. It worries me what will happen to him if I die first. I sometimes wonder what Ron thinks—how he thinks. Does his mind remember and he doesn't tell me—or is he forgetting even more and afraid to tell me. I hate Alzheimer's. How I wish I could turn back the clock and have Ron back—the Ron I knew— the Ron I married—the Ron I loved.

"Ron wanted to hug tonight. I swear he is the best hugger in the world. He sure hasn't forgotten how to do that. I love his hugs so much—I don't even want to think about never having his hugs. That's really going to hurt when that day comes—so I'm taking all of them that I can take now. I wish I could put them in a box and keep them for the future. I try and memorize the feel, while he is hugging me so I will never forget how special they are."

August found me taking our dog, Annie, to be groomed. I left her with the Groomer and would pick her up later in the day. When I returned home I saw Ron standing outside crying, almost trembling. I ran to see what was wrong. He just kept saying "I lost Annie, I lost Annie". He had forgotten I had taken her to be groomed and thought he had let her out and she had run away. I hugged him and reassured him she was okay. It continued to be hard for me to comprehend how in such a short time he had forgotten where I had gone. I made a promise I would never leave the house again without leaving him a note where I was.

Every once in a while there were normal days. Just when I thought nothing would ever be normal again, I would come home from work and find that Ron had gotten himself dressed, walked out to get the mail and was alert and talkative. Those were the moments that threw me more for a loop than when he was passive and quiet. It was during those moments that I wondered if I was imagining all the "other stuff" that was going on. Maybe he would snap out of this and be "my Ron" again. I began to learn there would be days, maybe only moments, when Ron would be Ron again. I needed to learn to just embrace those moments and enjoy them. Not expect any more than what they were—moments—but not ignore them either. Maybe God was allowing Ron back in my life for those moments so that I could appreciate them, hold them and tuck them away in my heart forever.

People have told me those who have Alzheimer's often have a change in taste buds or they crave one particular food all the time. Ron craved pasta. He would eat pasta every night if I let him. I suppose it wasn't good for me to give it to him all the time, but if it made him happy and he was filled by it, so what the heck.

Every morning I would ask Ron what he wanted for breakfast and every morning he would smile and say, "Gee, I haven't had a Burger King Egg and Sausage Sandwich in so long. That would taste really good.".

So every morning, Monday through Friday, Annie our dog, and I would take the pickup and drive to Burger King. Ron never remembered he had just had one the day before. I suppose it wasn't the most nutritional but at that point in my life that was the last thing on my mind.

Motor homing has become a challenge. We were back to having our motor home at our friends park. I enjoyed escaping for the weekends but Ron didn't handle it well. He didn't fit at the table in the motor home anymore so Frank removed it which gave him more room. Ron had trouble doing the steps to get into the motor home. I thought he would enjoy sitting outside during the day but he mostly chose to stay inside and sleep. After we were there for a day he wanted to come home. While we are motor homing with our friends—Ron has been really funny. Our friend, Frank, smokes Camel cigarettes. On the cigarette pack there is a camel on one side of the pack and a hotel on the other side. EVERY time Ron saw the cigarette pack he said to Frank "See that camel—what would you do if you were on that camel in the desert and didn't know where you were" and EVERY time Frank would say 'I don't know what should I do?" and Ron said as he flipped the pack over—"You ride the camel to the hotel and ask for directions." And than he would laugh and laugh. We would wait to see how many times in an evening he would tell this story. Frank was so kind. He acted as though it was the first time he had ever heard it every time Ron did it. If Ron told this story once he told it 100 times.

During the summer months we did have a few outings we were able to go to. We went to visit his children and grandchildren for a picnic. Ron enjoyed being with family. He was a grandfather to seven, Jordyn, Jessica, Paige, Brennan, Kyle, Jack and Kevin. He loved being "Grandpa Reed". He would still talk about things he planned to do with the grandchildren, taking Kyle fishing and our granddaughters camping. But now we couldn't stay any place long. I had learned as soon as we arrived someplace he wanted to leave.

Long trips and long days were a thing of the past for us. But if we could enjoy a few hours for a short drive or visit than I needed to accept that as our social life.

Chapter XIV

FALL—2002

Fall found Ron being diagnosed with Osteo Rheumatoid Arthritis in his wrist. The doctor insisted Ron should be on insulin and I agreed to take him to a Diabetic Specialist. Although I called in September the first appointment available was not until December. A four month wait! Our medical system is wonderful!

There are times when I felt as though I was walking this journey alone. At one of my support meetings I vented all of the fears I was feeling and the anger I felt inside. I ended by saying "Ron would hate the person he is becoming". One of the members of the support group looked at me and said "You are right—Ron would hate the person he is becoming—but he would Love the person you are becoming." I cannot tell you how that hit me. She was right. Ron would be proud I had chosen to accept this, stand by him and be his caregiver. He would love the person I was becoming. I knew I would carry that message with me in my heart for as long as this journey lasted.

No matter who the person is, your spouse, your child, your parent, grandparent or friend I hope you will remember also: "although they would hate who they are becoming—they would love who you are becoming through this journey with them".

The pages in my journal remained empty for two months. I wasn't sure why I stopped writing—sometimes I think it was because I was depressed. Other times I think it was because I was in denial and other times I think it was because I was in total acceptance. Does that make sense? The fall didn't bring major changes but I saw small progression with

Ron. He seemed to be less and less control of his bowels. Everywhere we went I took a "change bag" with us "just in case". I tried to not push panic buttons and tried to convince myself this wasn't something for me to be concerned about. But it's like this monster "Alzheimer's" would slam me with a "big One" as if to say—LOOK—I AM HERE—DEAL WITH ME.

One night I heard Ron trying to get to the bathroom and than heard him yelling and swearing and I knew he was in trouble. When I got to him I found him sitting on the toilet—except he had "forgotten" to pull his nightshirt up and had sat on his night shirt and gone to the bathroom. I lost my temper and starting yelling at him which did nothing but upset him more.

The hardest part for me to accept, I think, is that by the time I had gotten him out of the shower he had forgotten anything had taken place. We, the caregiver, do not forget—cannot forget. These are the things that will be embedded in our memory forever and I think that is what hurts most and is the hardest to accept. It is through moments like this I know this is not "my Ron"—this is not the person I married and not the person I knew. The worst part is Alzheimers has taken over his life. The best part is he forgets he has done something like this so it doesn't stay with him to be upset over.

Today Ron saw the Diabetes Specialist. The doctor began him on insulin. One shot every morning. The doctor showed me how to give the shot. I was never much of a "medical" person and I am very apprehensive, actually down right scared to have to give him shots. I came home today overwhelmed at this next "step" and my new role as caregiver.

Today I spent practicing on an orange on how to give a shot. That poor orange! I was angry, mad and scared. I am sick of all of this and I just want to run away and hide. For the first time on this journey I am the one saying "I can't do this".

It seemed every time I was ready to throw in the towel and "give up" someone would send me a saying or note that gave me the strength to keep going. So was the case now. I opened my email that day and found a friend had sent me the following:

You say "It's impossible"
God Says: All things are possible

You say "I'm too tired"
God Says: I will give you rest

You say "Nobody really loves me"
God Says: I Love You

You Say "I can't go on"
God Says: I will direct your steps

You Say "I can't do it"
God Says: You can do all things

You Say "I'm not able"
God Says: I am able

You Say "It's not worth it"
God Says: It will be worth it

You Say "I can't forgive myself"
God says : I'll forgive you

You Say "I can't manage"
God says" I will supply all your needs.

You say "I'm afraid"
God says: I have not given you a spirit of fear

You say "I'm worried and frustrated"
God Says: Cast all your care on Me

You say "I don't have enough faith"
God says: I've given everyone a measure of faith

You say "I feel all alone"
God says: I will never leave you or forsake you

I haven't written much about my faith but my faith is strong, and I believe God will see both Ron and I through this. Sometimes though I forget and think I have to do it all alone. I cannot explain it other than to say when I received this email I knew it would be okay and I would do what I had to do and do it right.

That night when it came time to give Ron his first shot I took a deep breath, asked God to help me steady the needle and I did it. I REALLY DID IT . . . And I did it well. It was as though God took my hand and led me through it. Sometimes I realize all too well that God has more faith in us than we do. So all is well—with pills and insulin we should be able to regulate his sugar. This was definitely a curve in the road on this journey but I know we made the turn and are headed in the right direction!!

"Christmas and Holidays!!! Can't I just go to bed, pull the covers over my head and wake up on January 2nd. There was no way I could do all the decorating and putting up the tree myself. So I hired someone to come and help me. Ron sat in his chair and watched. Last year he had been able to help me some but this year nothing. This is when I can monitor his progression—not from day to day—but from what he was able to do last year and this year."

The kids and grandchildren came to celebrate Christmas the Saturday before Christmas. It was a wonderful day. Ron appeared to be very much in the moment. He loved having his grandchildren here. It was a good day for all of us. By the time everyone left Ron was tired but happy.

Christmas Eve and Christmas Day were quiet, We watched old western movies on TV and Ron never knew it was Christmas. Christmas was just another day. I never mentioned Christmas nor did he. It was a long day but I survived it. I was glad when the holidays were over.

Chapter XV

WINTER 2003

A new year has arrived. Overall I would say the last year saw progression moderately. I would venture to guess that Ron moved from early stages Alzheimers to middle stages, however, I was very pleased as to how slow his progression was. It was now two years since all of this "hit the fan" and I never thought I would still have him as good as he is. So we will continue to take one day at a time.

"The first thing people will tell you is that as a caregiver you have to take time for yourself and take care of yourself. In the beginning I thought "well of course I will, why wouldn't I?" But as time goes on I find I am allowing myself less and less time for me and putting things I should be doing for me on the back burner. Only a care giver can understand how and why this happens and only a care giver can understand why it is so hard to allow ourselves the time we need. I think one reason is that by the time I have done everything for Ron I am just so tired. I don't want to take time for me. I just want to go to bed and sleep!"

"Today Ron woke up with the left side of his face swollen. I took him to the doctor and he has TMJ (which is the jaw joint that connects to the jaw). Tonight Ron asked why his face was swollen and I told him he has TMJ—I said "Do you know what TMJ is?" and he said "of course—Too much Jacci" I had to laugh—Sometimes that quick wit resurfaces for a moment and I love it!!!

Every morning when I wake up I wonder if this is going to be the day Ron doesn't know me. Every morning when I leave for work I kiss him goodbye and silently say goodbye to a little bit more of him. Every day when I come home from work I open the door and said "hello" to a little bit more of Alzheimers.

No one can walk this journey alone. I have been so blessed to have five people in my life who see me through each day. Anne and Frank, who have been my friends for many years, have not left me. When our area was struck by an ice storm and the electricity was out for days, Frank was here constantly making sure we were okay. Anne called every day and made sure I would find time for myself, even when I didn't want to. There are no words that can express the appreciation in my heart except to simply acknowledge them and say thank you. You are wonderful.

And there were three friends that became part of our lives. Three sisters Cheryl, Sandy and Julie walked every step of this journey with Ron and I from this point on. They came to be as much of this household as I was, doing and being everything for Ron. I don't have enough gratitude in my heart for these friends.

"It seems every day Ron is getting worse. He sleeps most of the days now. When he is awake he just sits and stares at the TV. He has no interest in going out and it's a struggle to get him to go on Saturdays for breakfast with his friends. I don't want to push panic buttons but my heart tells me something is happening. It isn't so much his memory as it is him physically. Sometimes I feel as though he's just sitting there slowly dying. How can this be? What am I suppose to do? What is going to happen six months from now? Spring is almost here. I was hoping we would have another summer to enjoy together. Will we? Sometimes the future scares me. I think today I will begin journaling in more detail, trying to track his daily activities more closely."

For years Ron would meet what I referred to as "his cronies" for breakfast. Four men, all retired, who would meet at "Pete's", a local restaurant at exactly 10:00 am, have breakfast, discuss the world news, and their points of views. Saturdays, the wives were invited to join this breakfast "club" and soon we all became friends. Phil and Barb, Ron and Kay, Ed and Jeanne, Ron and I. This was one of the last things Ron would still agree to do. He so enjoyed these "buddies" and as he could not drive anymore, Saturday was the only day he would see them. But as the weeks went by, each Saturday found me struggling a bit more to get him up and agreeable to go. Once there he was fine, but getting him there was a nightmare. It was at this point I knew for sure "something" was changing. He was losing interest in his favorite event of the week. What was going on in his mind? His body?

At this point I would be remiss if I didn't mention Ron's best friend in his life, Don. Don and Ron had been friends for 65 years. I couldn't imagine having a best friend for that long. They are like two "peas in a pod". I could sit for hours listening and laughing about their "escapades" when they were younger. They were "brothers" in every sense of the word. It hurt Don to see Ron having to go through this. He was losing his friend and it was hard.

Chapter XVI

SPRING 2003

There was a retirement incentive offered at my work and I retired the end of March. This was perfect timing. I hoped that my being home would help Ron to want to get up and about a little bit more.

It would be hard for me to stop working. My career had been with the New York State Department of Labor for thirty seven years. I was a Supervisor in a rural employment office with seven employees. We had become more than co-workers, we were friends, we were extended family to each other. They were my comfort zone. They listened to me, cried with me, laughed with me, encouraged me, counseled me and supported me. The thought of not having them available to me every day was scary. There will forever be a special place in my heart for Mitch, Vicki, Monica, Lalo, Nancy, Nan and Chris

Being home gave me time to clean closets, the garage, the basement. It was not until after it was done that I realized something more important had happened. All that "stuff" that I was throwing out were "memories" of our life together. And I thought how much easier it was for me to go through those things while Ron was still here with me than it would be for me to have to go through them after he died. When we lose someone we love and we have to start "cleaning out" it is extremely hard emotionally and mentally.

Everything we touch has a memory and connection. But by cleaning out our house while Ron was still alive I wasn't throwing away a part of him, I was just throwing away "stuff." I remember when I found the suit he wore when we were married I just shook my head and laughed. Had I had to do this after he died it would have been emotionally traumatic for me. As a fulltime caregiver for a terminally ill loved one, I would suggest you try this. It will keep you busy and it will be so much easier for you to do while they are alive.

April found Ron experiencing more and more difficulty getting out of chairs. He had no strength in his wrists at all and at over 300 pounds it was hard for him to get up. About 95 percent of the time he had to call me to get him up which worries me. What if I wasn't home when he needed to get up. I decided to buy him a lift chair. I was injuring my hip by yanking him up and was using a cane to walk. So much for the care giver taking care of herself.

"Today Ron saw his Primary Doctor. He had gained fifteen pounds and now weighs 340. He can hardly walk and is off balance when he does. He gasps for air if he takes more than fifteen steps at a time. I met with the doctor privately the next day. Doctor Johnson feels Ron is failing more quickly physically than he is mentally. The Aricept has really kept his AD at status quo but physically his body is beginning to simply shut down. By not moving and not being active his bones and muscles are beginning to deteriorate. His vision is getting worse, he has lost all strength in his wrists and legs which is causing him to be off balance. He simply wants to sit, sleep and eat. In Doctor Johnson's opinion it is likely Ron will not live more than six to twelve months. He spent a lot of time with me discussing the symptoms of stroke, congestive heart failure, blood clots and advising me what I will need to look for and be aware of from this time on. I walked away from this visit knowing I have turned the corner on this disease and entering a new level. I am not prepared for this. But I also know the Doctor is right. Ron is failing more physically than mentally. I just haven't allowed myself to see it."

"It is time for me to take stock of this new stage and how I am going to handle it. I know the first thing I need to do is begin to release Ron and let him be and do what he wants. I have to stop forcing him to be part of my world and have to start trying

to find a place in his. I have to stop "setting him up to fail". By making him go places he doesn't want to go or making him do things he can no longer do, all I am doing is setting him up to fail at it. If he wants to sit and sleep than I need to allow him to do that. I have to face the reality of what is and not what I would like it to be."

"I feel as though I am a widow with a living husband. Does that make sense? Our "friends" have already begun to treat me differently. We're not invited to parties and social events with "friends" anymore. I think probably they're embarrassed of Ron and feel awkward inviting me without a partner. I have begun to try and learn how to do things alone. I'm a caregiver. I need to be here to take care of Ron and see him through this. I love him. I always will. But I have to begin to let him go. He is leaving me and I need to allow him to do that. It will be easier down the road if I take these steps now".

When I went to my support group they talked about vision and how it affects Alzheimer's. I never realized it but AD patients experience vision problems. They are not caused by the eye but rather by the brain. A person with AD can have difficulty perceiving what he sees rather that how sharply he sees it. AD patients experience vision problems in four areas: motion, depth, color and contrast. Of course, not every person experiences the same problems, some have no problems other have one or more. The group leader told us it was important that we, as caregivers, understand what people with AD may be seeing when they look at an object and how that differs from what the caregiver is seeing when they are looking at the same object. Some folks with AD are even unable to sense movement—things that are moving actually look like they are standing still which is why they can lose balance or trip over things. Things that have depth may look flat to them and they may trip over them without realizing it. Colors fade on them. The color red seems to remain the brightest, so they suggest that we use red to highlight items we want to make sure the person sees. Putting higher wattage in light bulbs can also help as the brighter the light the better they will see. As I thought about this it may be the reason why Ron has tripped over the steps going from the family room to the upper level. They may appear "flat" to him and he doesn't know to lift his leg to go up the step.

I found few people who understood the moment to moment, day to day life when AD has made its way into your life. As a caregiver I found myself going above and beyond to do what I had to do to retain dignity in Ron's life and to make him as "normal" as possible when with others—including family and friends. Family and friends were the first to say to me "they understood," but when an incident happened, you could see in their eyes the fear, the embarrassment and the desire to leave as soon as possible. Alzheimers to them was sitting watching a loved one say silly things or pretend they're someone they are not. I found every moment of my life was involved with Ron. Even when I was gone for a few hours, I was never really far from him. I was constantly making sure my cell phone was on so he could call—looking at my watch to make sure I hadn't been gone too long, wondering if he had fallen and couldn't get up. It never left me. Simply leaving the house—leaving the person didn't allow me to leave the concern. Ron had a lot of pride—most of our loved ones do—and to have a stranger come into the house to bathe, feed, and dress them—they react hostile and become angry and abusive. I got to "know" how to do things and get things done without a struggle. You control their lives and you do it out of love and survival. They come to depend on you to do this without even knowing it. Ron had no idea when he took pills or what pills he took—I just gave them to him and he took them. He had no idea when to shower or how he got dressed or how his feet had lotion on them. I just did those things for him and they were done. He didn't know when he ate or what he had eaten. I fixed all his meals and served him and he ate it and was filled.

"I must be very careful when I take Ron out in public now. He's beginning to say inappropriate things to people he meets, especially women. I have noticed lately he tries to act sexual but in a bad manner. It's almost like he is groping at me. This is so

uncharacteristic for Ron. I can handle it and know this isn't "him" but strangers don't know him and are offended by his actions and comments. I know it will not be long before I will not be able to take him out in public."

"When the doctors tell me to get a grip—"get a life"—where and when do I do that. How can I enjoy myself on a cruise knowing he is here alone—with a stranger washing him and caring for him and he hating every moment that I am not here? I am his care giver—he depends on me—I am his security—his comfort—his protector. He trusts me and he allows me to do the personal things that need to be done. He knows I will never tell anyone what I have to do for him—he knows I will allow him to live in dignity and stature with his friends and family. I know he gets really anxious when I'm not with him—he's afraid when he is alone. How could I leave him for a "vacation?"

My retirement totally confused Ron. He had no idea I had retired although I told him continuously. Every day he would say "It must be Saturday because you're home." The first week I kept correcting him, than I just let it be and every day became Saturday. My being home didn't increase his desire to get up and about. He had no desire to get up dressed or go anywhere.

May found me trying desperately to get Ron out to motor home. Once again Frank set up our motor home on their extra lot at Leisurewood Park. It was a beautiful lot and Frank was meticulous about maintaining it. One evening Ron and I joined Anne and Frank for a campfire. Seriously speaking, Ron began to tell Frank that eventually we'd have to sell our motor home "and lot" and he wanted Frank to know he would offer to sell it to Frank first. Frank thanked him and told him he would consider it. We all laughed after, this was Frank's lot. How kind it was for Ron to offer to sell Frank his own lot!

I found significant changes in motor homing this year. In May, I bought Ron a golf cart knowing he wouldn't be able to walk and hoping that we could, at least, enjoy the fresh air and new environment. Every time he would see the golf cart parked in our lot he would ask who it belonged to. When I told him it was his, he got a big smile on his face and said "I have a golf cart?

Ron was only agreeable to be at the motor home for a few hours, always wanting to come home. I agreed as it was apparent his inability to walk, stand and sit comfortably was making him restless and anxious. He simply wanted to be at home all the time now.

"Today was an exceptionally good day. We went to a family picnic out of town which turned into a surprise retirement party for me. Ron did pretty well although we did experience an "incident" from eating way too many desserts. Thankfully our family is compassionate and understanding through these "times". The family hasn't been together for a while so it was a great day to enjoy.

On the way home to keep Ron busy we sang "old love songs". Ron still has such a nice voice and knew every word to all the old songs. It was like having back a "moment in time" with Ron, the man I knew, the man I loved, the man that made me laugh. It is as though he comes back to me for just a moment and than leaves me again. I embrace the moment and than grieve it when it is over."

Chapter XVII

Summer 2003

The first week of July found Ron experiencing excruciating pain in his right leg. He was not able to stand or put pressure on it. Cheryl, Sandy and Julie came and helped me take him to the emergency room. When they tried to take him for x-rays he started getting nasty with the technician, who then came in with a needle.

"What is that for?" Ron snapped. The technician promptly replied smiling "This, Mr Reed is going to make you nicer to me!"

The x-rays showed no breaks or fractures. The diagnosis of his pain was sciatica. I went home and converted our bedroom into a nursing room. I had a hospital bed delivered, brought up his lift chair and put our big TV into our room. The two days it took to make these changes were trying days for Ron. There were too many changes and too much commotion. He didn't do well.

On the third day he was in so much pain he couldn't get up out of the chair. Sandy, Julie, Cheryl and I decided to call 911 for the paramedics to come and take him to the hospital. Both of our volunteer fire departments also answered the call. Ron refused to go to the hospital. He became nasty and loud. One of the fireman called the police. When an officer arrived he suggested perhaps he could convince him to go to the hospital. I agreed. When the police officer walked into the bedroom Ron became threatening.

"Do you think just because you have a uniform and a gun you are going to make me get up. I have more guns in this house than all of you put together" Ron yelled.

Well, in this day and age you don't make remarks like that—and the officer called for backup. Within five minutes I had five police cars in my driveway—One police officer interrogating me in the dining room on where "our weapons" were. I finally convinced them the closest thing I have to a weapon is a paring knife in the kitchen. The bottom line was that if Ron didn't agree to go they couldn't make him go. And he wasn't about to. So I had to let everyone leave and deal with him myself. If you ever wanted to know what a day from hell was—this was my day from hell.

Weeks went by with Ron never leaving the bedroom. He developed a bed sore (or what I referred to as a chair sore). Dr. Johnson felt it was time to have a home health nurse and physical therapist come twice a week. I felt better knowing he was being monitored professionally. The biggest problem arose when Ron would become totally alert and agreeable with the nurse and therapist. When it was just he and I he didn't do anything. He went into the "I can't" mode with me continuously. "I can't get out of the chair, I can't get into the bed, I can't cut my meat, I can't walk to the bathroom" Everything was a struggle. But when the nurse and therapist were here he was a totally different person.

"Mr, Reed, can you get out of the chair for me" they would ask.

"Sure, no problem" he would say.

"Mr Reed, can you walk for me" they would ask. Ron was unbelievable. He got out of the chair like grease lightening. He walked to the kitchen counter—up the step without hesitation. The therapist wanted him to go down the four stairs to the family room. He hasn't been in the family room for two months.

"I don't think he can," I said.

"Sure I can," Ron said and took off down the stairs.

Only using the railing he was down the steps in a heart beat. I just stared in disbelief. I just looked at him and said "Who are you and what did you do with Ron!" The therapist laughed and said "You know the patients will always do more for us than they will their families".

"I guess so," I snapped. Well—now I don't know what to think. Is Ron perfectly okay and just playing that he can't get around? Is he sometimes okay and sometimes not okay? What is all of this about?

This same routine went on when folks came to visit. In front of them he was "normal as could be". Only my closest friends and family believed the life I was living. The rest of the world thought I was exaggerating his condition and making more out of his illness than I had to. I believe now that Ron had enough presence of mind to believe if he could convince everyone he was "fine," than no one would encourage me to have him placed in long term care. More than anything in his life, he wanted to stay at home, he wanted to die at home.

"My world feels alone and dark. Ron is existing in a world he no longer knows. I am learning it is harder to live in darkness with someone than in a world of light alone. Does that make sense?"

Ron sat in his lift chair 24 hours a day. His chair was about five feet from the bathroom and it was a struggle to get him in there. It took him about 10 minutes to get to the bathroom with his walker and he screamed in pain all the way.

More than once he would try to walk and lose his balance. He would get up in the middle of the night, try to walk and end up falling. Eventually it got to the point where I couldn't pull him up and the paramedics came to know our address as well as their own. Remarkably, he never hurt himself and an hour later he had forgotten the entire ordeal.

It was at this time I bought a baby monitor so I could hear him if I were in another room. This made it so much easier for me to monitor him and not have to be with him every minute.

Chapter XVIII

Fall 2003

"Fall is here already. I don't remember summer being here. I sometimes think I live in a "fog". I'm no longer up to date on news events. The world is going by me and I'm removed from it. My world is here. It's a very small world! The leaves are already beginning to change. I think it's going to be a short fall. I dread winter coming.

These days I dread just about everything! What I'm dealing with most these days is guilt. It's so hard for me to write about this because I feel ashamed and weak. But the truth is, dear journal, that I am just so tired.

Tired of all of this. And what I grieve most is for my life-not Ron's. I mean he is "comfortable" "satisfied" with his life. He doesn't miss "living" and he is at peace just sitting and letting life go by. His pain comes only when he goes to stand up and the only time he stands up is when he has to go to the bathroom, maybe three to four times a day. So for maybe one hour a day he has pain—but the other twenty three hours he's happy and content. He has everything at his beck and call and he has no memory he even has a problem. He watches television, he sleeps and he eats. I, on the other hand have to deal with all of life's daily events for both of us. I listen to his every breath. I wait on him a hundred times a day. I never leave this house. I sit and watch my life dying right along with his. I cannot imagine what good God sees in all of this. All it is—is just plain pain."

"I fear the end is coming soon. I try and prepare myself for it and yet I know in so many ways I haven't prepared at all. What is hardest for me is seeing him suffer and deteriorate before my eyes. Every day he seems to get worse. I have prayed for answers and I can only hope that God has heard me and will answer my prayers. People around me are telling me that I really need to make the decision and have him put in a nursing home. "it will be best for him and you." I don't agree.

Ron is my "other half", my soul mate. I love him with all that I have within me. I am not against nursing homes and it isn't that I would not consider it when it is necessary. But the truth is right now I can take care of Ron. Yes, it is a lot of work and yes it is scary, but there isn't anything that he needs that I can't do for him now. People say he is taking away my life but they don't understand that he is my life and if he leaves, a part of my life leaves me also. The reality is that if I put him in a nursing home today it would be because he was interfering with my life, my freedom. And that isn't the reason I can accept. If he becomes so bad I can no longer care for him. If he becomes violent or threatening or if he doesn't know me or know this house than that will be different. Than the nursing home is the best place for him. But today he knows me, he remembers he loves me, and he needs to be with me. Yes, this is hard and long and sad but if death is a part of life than my mission—my promise to Ron—is to be there with him through his transition."

It is September and I called Hospice to come out to do an evaluation on Ron. They felt he was not "ready" for Hospice yet. He was so alert with them and so much in the moment. Everything they asked him to do, he did.

They did arrange for a home health nurse to come out and monitor him. They assured me that when the Nurse felt he met the qualifications for Hospice she would notify them and he would be admitted into their program. By telling me he was "not ready" for Hospice and knowing Hospice accepts you when they feel you are in your last six months, I had to reassess my gut feelings if, in fact, he was beginning his dying process. But never having been a care giver and never having cared for a dying person I now convinced myself I was wrong and Ron had many months to live yet.

"I made a decision to look at Ron as a different identity in my life. I realize these past weeks I have become resentful of him and I hate that. I resented his not being the man I married, the man I loved, the man I want in my life. I looked at him and saw" Ron" and forgot this disease had taken away the identity of "Ron". The reality was the body lives but the man I loved, I knew, I wanted no longer lives within that body. Ron remembers who I am, but no longer remembers our life together. I feel as though I'm a page in the chapter of his life but the only writing on the page is my name. I wonder how long it will be before he will no longer even see my name and all there will be before him is a blank page. Alzheimer's has taken over control of his body and his mind. It's hard to say these things let alone accept them. I want and need to continue to care for him. So this week I changed his name to "Al". Now I am caring for "Al". Why "Al" you ask??? Why not, Alzheimer's is winning—it might as well have the name to the body it has taken control over. From now on Ron will be AKA "Al Zimer". In my mind I can scream to Al I hate him, resent him. I can deal with "Al" and I will. "My Ron" is not to blame for this hell and I will not allow this disease to destroy my love for Ron."

By the middle of September I was needed to be with Ron 24/7. He could do nothing for himself. I served his meals to him in his chair. I took him to the bathroom, cleaned him and dressed him. Showering I had a shower chair which made the process easy. It was such a struggle to get him to agree to let me give him a shower, but once in there he felt so good and wanted to stay there forever that it was worth it.

"I cry more than I laugh, I write more than I talk. Everyone tells you to take care of yourself. Don't let your loved one destroy your life also. But how do you do that and what do they mean? Would they do the same thing if they were walking in our shoes? I know for certain that five years ago I would never have believed I would be in the position I am today. I had little patience and a lot of independence. Care giving was not something I thought about, wanted or would agree to exist in my life. And yet here I sit wondering not so much how Ron will survive, because I know he will not, but rather how I will survive. The reality is I want to take care of myself, but I need to take care of Ron and I don't have the strength to do both. One of us has to suffer and it has to be me. In my support group everyone feels the same and that is why I have included this in my journal. For so long I thought this was just me. But it is not. We do just enough to make sure we don't get seriously ill and we put all of the rest of our energy into care giving. As one woman said, "If my husband only knew what my life was like and what I have sacrificed because it is so important for me to allow him to live and die in love and dignity". And we all cried and hugged because it was true for all of us."

"I ordered Ron a hospital bed the first week in July—over eight weeks ago—and he has refused to get into it. His bedsore is terrible. Tonight I finally got him into the hospital bed. As soon as he gets in bed he says "I need a glass of water" so I get up and get him a glass of water. I lay down and I hear, "I need a Kleenex" so up I go and get him a Kleenex. My head doesn't hit the pillow when he says "Where's my urinal". Just like a child fighting bedtime. When he realized this was not going to get to me he became quiet and I finally thought sleep was ahead for me.

I was just dozing off when I start to hear him screaming "GET ME OUT OF HERE!! I WANT TO GET OUT OF HERE!! LET ME OUT NOW". The railings were up on both sides of the bed and he couldn't get out. I pretended not to hear him. He yelled louder—swearing and screaming to high heaven, "When I get out of here I am going to kill you" and I had to smile thinking "that's a real incentive for me to get up and bring down the rails!

After a few minutes of his yelling I got up. "OKAY" I started "enough is enough. You can get out of bed and sit in your chair. I'm done with you and I'm done trying to help you.

I got him in the chair and marched over to my bed and laid down. I could see him sitting there, he was crying but not moving. I let him be. Finally I went to sleep. About two hours later I woke up and looked in the chair to check on him. The chair was empty—where was he?—what did I do? I got up, and there he was IN THE HOSPITAL BED sleeping like a baby. Here he had gotten up by himself, and into bed by himself. I will never understand this disease—it just baffles me all the time."

Chapter XIX

Dying Well

Birth is a beginning—Death is a destination.

The most difficult thing in the world to do is to sit, listen and wait while your loved one is dying.

When I knew Ron was beginning his dying process, I knew I had to begin to prepare myself and Ron as we began to live out the last chapter in his life.

This was a time when I learned the difference about "giving up" and "letting go." Ron was not giving up. He had fought this disease for three years. He had tried his hardest to stay in this world. But he was tired now.

He wanted rest. He wanted the pain over and he wanted to know it was okay for him to die. He wasn't giving up—he was letting go. Letting go of Alzheimers. Letting go to God. Letting go to acceptance of his dying. This didn't have to be the saddest time of his life.

Birth was his beginning, Death was his destination.

Our loved ones need a "sacred space" to die in. Whether they're in a hospital, nursing home or family home, they need "their space," their comfort zone. For Ron, his lift chair became his ***sacred space***. This was the place he felt most secure, restful, peaceful and safe.

He would sleep, eat, live and die in his chair. He would say his goodbyes to family and friends from that chair. He would hold his grandchildren in that chair for the last time. I would sit next to him for hours and talk about our life and our love for each other. We laughed, we cried, we remembered in his sacred space. It was in his chair that I told him it was okay for him to die. That I would be okay. That his children and grandchildren would be okay. It was from that chair that he gave me his last kiss. It was from this chair that we prayed together and it was from this chair that we said goodbye together. His *sacred space* became my sacred space and it became spiritual and holy. He had shared his life with me, now he was about to share his death with me. What greater bond of love exists.

Chapter XX

THE LAST SIX WEEKS

It was September. Fall was beginning to fill the air. Summer had come and gone in the blink of an eye. Where had the time gone? What was ahead for Ron and I?

I read extensive articles on the dying process. I needed to know what to expect in the days and weeks ahead of us. I had always feared death and the notion that it could be a peaceful and fulfilling part of life boggled my mind. Research lead me to learning about death and how our physical and spiritual bodies react to it. The more I read the more intrigued I became. Two separate identities disconnecting from this world—our physical body and our spiritual body. Allowing the person time to prepare for their "disconnect" and find their way through their transition. It was all new and nervously anticipating for me. When I wondered why Ron was sleeping so many of his days away, I learned this was time he was "preparing" spiritually to disconnect from this world. Time spent in earthly issues still unresolved. Time spent feeling his way slowly into the next world so he would have a smooth and easy transition. It was suggested in many articles not to insist on waking the person. Allowing them to be where they needed to be for as along as they needed to be there. When they awake and come back into our world, embrace the moment and enjoy them and than allow them to leave back into that other world in sleep when they need to. And so I did. Ron would sleep for hours straight, wake up for a hour or two and be very much in the moment, then drift back into that deep sleep for hours again. This went on for days.

Than came the change in appetite. Always being a food lover and always overweight, it was apparent that things were changing within him when he lost his appetite. For ten days he refused to eat and drank very little. At first I was alarmed and tried forcing him to eat and drink. Back to the research articles. There was no need to force him to eat or drink. This was a normal reaction of the body in the dying process stage. The body no longer needed food—It no longer wanted food. Allowing the body to prepare itself for death the way it was intended. And so I did. I did not force food into him. I gave him enough fluid to make him comfortable but did not force more than he needed or wanted.

It was during the second week that Ron asked me "What is going on with me? Why am I feeling like this? Am I sick?" And I knew I had to be honest and direct with him. We always had been and now more than ever

I needed to let him be a part of his dying process.

The hardest words I ever spoke were "Honey, your body is getting very tired and it is beginning to simply shut down. You are starting what they call the dying process."

"What does that mean?" he asked and I simply answered "It means that eventually your body is going to stop functioning and you are going to die". He cried, I cried. I held him in my arms. "Isn't there a pill they can give me? Isn't there something I can do?" he whispered with tears in his eyes. "I don't think so, it is too late. But I promise you I will be here with you and we will walk through this together hand in hand"

Today I arranged to have his children, grandchildren, mother, brothers and sisters, nieces and nephews come and see him. One by one he spent time with them. Having personal conversations and saying goodbye to each of them. I was so proud of him. He was so strong and so in control. Even with his Alzheimer's working against him, he was able to remember the times he needed to remember with them and say what he wanted to say to them. He told his Grandson Kyle, to remember that he would always be with him—to always remember that. And I will never forget Nicholas with a quivering voice standing before Ron saying, "I love you Uncle Ron and I'm going to miss you, and have a nice trip to Heaven." Today the family was sitting around him talking and laughing and filling the room with love. Each of his children spent quiet moments alone with him, sharing what only needed to shared between them. I will always remember our granddaughter Jessica sitting on his lap and hugging him. I will remember the vision of his mother sitting next to him and thinking how painful it must be for her to know her son was dying. The reality is that Alzheimer's at this moment has become his friend. Once the day was over so was the memory of it and he never had to relive the memories of saying his goodbyes.

The third week he woke up starving and wanting a full breakfast. I was ecstatic. Perhaps this was a miracle. Perhaps his body had "changed its mind" and was not going to die. For five days he ate normal and was back to living. Life was beginning to make sense again.

But just as soon as I thought we were heading in the right direction, he did a complete turn around and stopped eating. This time would be the last time. I had heard that sometimes one can go through this sequence four or five times. For Ron it was only once.

It was now the first week of October. The next four days changed my life. For four straight days, twenty four hours a day, Ron did nothing but talk while in deep sleep. He would "pick the air" lifting his arms up into the air and putting his two fingers together as though grabbing at something in the air. Researchers suggest that this be interpreted as their trying to prioritize events throughout their life. Also, he would take the edge of his blanket and roll it up with his fingers and than unroll it, doing this over and over. But the most fascinating experience was just sitting there listening. He would talk non stop. Always as though he was carrying on a conversation with someone. Much was in a mumble state which couldn't be understood, but much was clear and precise. I laid on the bed for four days just listening to him and writing down word for word what he talked about. He talked to family and friends who had already crossed over through death. He acknowledged his Aunt Marion and said to her "Thank you Aunt Marion, I know you do,"

Aunt Marion had died of Alzheimer's a few years prior and it's my hope that she was here to help him understand what he had and that he would no longer have that once he passed. Here are some of the other "conversations" that Ron encountered:

"What did you just stick me with? Did you just pull it out? It hurts! What?

"Barb, that isn't right, don't do that"

"Buzzy is doing what? Don't let her do that!"

"Say what? He don't want to do that"

"It isn't that easy Tom. I think he should go to Idaho"

"It's okay to turn the switch on and you'll have more light" (I actually thought Ron was talking to me and I asked him why he wanted me to turn the light on. At that point he responded "Not you, the person who is standing in the doorway")

"Jacci, why is this girl here tonight? Why is she here with us tonight? Is she going to stay here all night?" (When I asked who she was, there was no answer)

"No, I can't. I'm sick—I'm really sick. Just leave me be for now"

"What do you want me to do? I don't swear. What do you want from me. Wow you are strong. Don't make me do that. What am I suppose to do?"

"What am I suppose to be spraying? I don't want to.

Why do I have to?"

"I still feel it moving. Don't wait, tell them now"

"Who are you dancing with? Oh!

"Geez you showed up so fast. (He began laughing hysterically and than said "yep"

"Who will determine what we do or make"

"So long, so far"

"I swear that's what she said"

"I can see some down there! THERE! THERE! NO! THERE (he was yelling very loudly)

"Leave it, I don't see it. Go ahead of me"

"This Burger King lady reminds me of a show girl" (He was laughing)

"How do you do that? Sure. Okay. Whatever"

(Pointing into the air with his finger) "YOU! YOU! YOU! Can stay—the rest of you have to leave."

"I think what we should do is take a vote on what we should do"

"Cliff? I don't know him"

"Oh, so you put the little red guy in the little red hole and the little black guy in the little black hole"

"You leave my son David alone, No one talks down and dirty to David. I'll take care of you—you &*&! You understand? You understand? David will take care of it—that's that! (David is Ron's son)

"Turn that yellow flash light on"

"Look at the sky—Oh my goodness it goes forever"

"Colleen, you always do what's right for daddy—you're good for daddy!" (Colleen is Ron's daughter)

"Jesus, pull up a stool and sit with me"

"We have to get all the children and put them in the hand of God'

"The last thing I have to do is turn the light on in the steeple"

"I can't open the door, Is someone there?"

"Nobody understand nobody here"

"Just when I am ready to go I wake up again. Back and forth. Back and Forth. (Ron was crying when he said this)

"I'm telling you, you gotta get your ass kicked before you can kick ass"

"I'm a good cook. I'm a great cook. I love to cook.

What do you want? Hot Dogs or Beans?"

"All I want is my chair and my clothes"

And then there were other moments. One time at 2:00 am Ron woke me out of a sound sleep singing at the top of his voice "THE HILLS OF KENTUCKY ARE WHERE I'LL LIVE FOREVER".

We never lived in Kentucky but Ron would go there every year for three weeks to volunteer for Habitat. He sang this line over and over. One night laying peacefully quiet he began speaking fluently in French. Ron had learned French while in French Morocco during the Korean War but I never heard him speak it fluently. He carried on "a conversation" in French for over ten minutes. It was simply amazing to witness this.

Throughout all of these conversations he would stop in between remarks as though someone was saying something to him. These were not hallucinations. Ron was not on any pain medications. Not even aspirin.

This was the spirit working in full force.

Much of his conversations were connected with building. His remarks were as though he was giving direction or instruction. Ron was in construction all of his life. I told him once when he was awake that I thought he was starting to "rebuild heaven" and that perhaps he might want to wait until he actually gets there before he starts giving orders. But that was so typical of Ron.

Sometimes I felt as though I had so many souls in my bedroom I wondered if there was any room left for me. And yet none of this was scary or threatening or even eerie. For some reason it just seemed "natural" and safe. It wasn't upsetting to Ron so it was not upsetting to me.

After four continuous days of this, it stopped as fast as it began. The talking was done and from that point on Ron pretty much just slept. No food and very little fluids.

Chapter XXI

The Final Days

On October 8th Ron's visiting nurse came and Ron was quiet. I told the nurse about his "conversations", his change of appetite, his picking the air with his fingers. I told her I knew "something is going on but I don't know what to do." She stayed with me for a long time and just listened. When I was through she looked at me and said simply, "It is time for Hospice".

"I tried to get Hospice to accept him a month ago but they said he wasn't ready" I said.

"Let me call them and talk to them. It is much harder when you are dealing with Alzheimer's patients. We have to rely on family members to help us diagnose."

The following day I was contacted by Hospice and Karen came out to visit Ron and I. Ron was having a good day and I thought for sure she would tell me I was crazy and not accept him into their program.

After spending time with Ron and talking with me she told me she would recommend that Ron be accepted into Hospice.

"I have to be honest with you" Karen told me. "Just talking with Ron today he doesn't fit into our time frame, but I am taking the information given by the visiting nurse and the facts that you tell me have been happening over the past week. Once our team becomes involved with Ron and you on a personal level we will be able to assess his needs better."

Tonight as I write in my journal I am relieved. Having Hospice involved now I do not have to worry about doctors or scheduling nursing visits. I will have 24 hour assistance. I feel a huge weight

has been lifted off my shoulders. Hospice will provide us with Doctors, Nurses, Counseling, Spiritual Assistance, Support Groups and so much more. By late afternoon I had delivered to me a box of medications that I am to keep in the refrigerator and not open unless instructed to by the Doctor or Nurse. I have no idea what they are for but I feel good having them. They have already placed a notice on our bedroom door that reads DNR (Do Not resuscitate) and I have been given phone numbers to call if I need assistance 24 hours a day. I think I will sleep tonight."

On Saturday October 11, I was laying on our bed, Ron was sleeping. He woke up crying calling for me. I went to him and sat next to him holding his had.

"I saw my dad," he said. "I really saw my dad".

Ron's dad had died in 1958. "He was right here, standing at the foot of my chair and he talked to me. He asked me what was wrong. He asked me if I was okay? There were a line of people I didn't know walking behind him. I couldn't see their faces or even their bodies but yet I knew they were people. It was strange. He told me it was okay, everything will be okay".

Than Ron turned his head toward me and with tears streaming down his face he said, "And Jacci, I saw IT, I saw IT."

"What did you see Ron?" I asked.

He just said over again "I saw IT! It is beautiful, like firecrackers—No—like brilliant colors I've never seen, No that's not it either. I can't describe it, but I saw IT."

I streaked my fingers through his hair and said "You saw a glimpse of Heaven didn't you?" and he sobbed and nodded saying only one more time "I saw IT."

Later than night he told me once again about his glimpse of Heaven. This time he told me "I was always afraid of dying. I never thought I was a good enough man to be with God. But now I know I was and I'm not afraid anymore".

And I knew that at that moment he had made his disconnect from this world spiritually. Now it was only a waiting game until his body was ready to disconnect.

When the nurse came on Monday, Ron was awake and alert. Hospice has taken him off all of his medications now. They are monitoring him very carefully.

How can you begin to explain what this organization does to allow a person to die with dignity and with peace. Because of them and with them, I knew I would be able to walk these last "steps" with Ron.

For the next three days Ron was in deep sleep most of the time. It was as though he had one foot in this world and one foot in the next. It became more and more apparent that he preferred "the next world" and would only sneak back into our world for an hour or so from time to time. The time he was awake I treasured. It was during those moments that I embraced every hug, every word, every last memory I could create. I knew time was running out and there was nothing I could do but just love him and let him go.

Thursday, October 16, Ron woke me with the excitement of a child on Christmas Day.

"I saw Aunt Viv," he said.

Aunt Viv was a special aunt who had always been an important part of Ron's life. She had died nine years ago. It had perplexed me through his four day "conversations" that he had never seen his Aunt Vivian. I wondered how someone so important in someone's life would not be there when all these other people were.

"What did she say to you?" I asked.

"She was smiling and telling me she was there and waiting for me to come".

Somehow it all made sense to me now. All these other people were *preparing Ron for his transition*, Aunt Viv was *waiting for Ron to make his transition.* The clock was ticking and time was running out.

Friday, October 17, found Ron very restless. He was awake most of the day. Not in pain but breathing restlessly. He was going farther into his other world and I knew our time together would soon be over. I laid on the bed next to his chair listening to his every breath and waiting for the next one to happen.

In the silence of the day he woke up and said "Jacci are you here?"

"Yes honey I am here" I said..

"Jacci, I want you to know that I love you more than anyone I have ever loved in my life. Always remember that!"

Somehow I found the strength to respond "I know and I love you too sweetie—always remember that."

That night he became more restless. I called Cheryl and she came to sit with me. When she went into check on Ron and woke him he was angry with her.

"GET OUT OF HERE! LEAVE ME ALONE." Ron yelled.

Hospice had instructed me that if Ron went over 12 hours without urinating I should contact them. It had been over 16 hours and because of his restlessness Cheryl convinced me to call Hospice. I was hesitant as it was almost 10:00 pm.

"That's what they are there for." Cheryl said.

I finally agreed and called Hospice. A nurse was sent over immediately.

Trying to prepare Ron that the nurse was coming he screamed at me "YOU WOMEN ARE MAKING ME MAD. LEAVE ME ALONE!".

When the nurse came she began to make preparation to place a catheter into Ron. He resisted and asked why he needed one.

"Your wife tells me you have not urinated in over sixteen hours"

"I can urinate if I want to" Ron said. "If you want me to urinate I will urinate"

The nurse looked at me and I just shrugged my shoulders.

"Okay Ron" I said. Let's see if you can go to the bathroom.

I helped him get up and although it took him a long time to walk, he did make it into the bathroom. Dumbfounded I stood there as he peed like a horse into the toilet. I could not believe my eyes.

After getting him back into his chair he looked at the nurse and said "See, I don't need a catheter".

I don't know if I was more embarrassed or angry. The nurse just looked at me like I was absolutely crazy.

Trying to redeem myself I said, "Well he has refused to drink a drop of liquid all day."

Looking at Ron, the nurse asked "Is that true?"

Ron just blatantly responded "Well, if someone would bring me some Root Beer I would drink it."

The nurse looked at me and asked "Do you have Root Beer?"

"Yes I do" I snapped sarcastically. "And I will be more than happy to get your some."

Knowing for certain that he would not drink it I went to kitchen and poured the largest glass we had of ice cold Root Beer, took it into him and watched as he drank every last drop. I just stood there totally dumbfounded.

"Well" the nurse said. "I think you are doing just fine".

As she was packing up her case to leave Ron said "Can I ask you something?"

"Of course she said, you can ask me anything".

"Well" Ron continued "Jacci tells me I am in a dying process. Am I starting to die?"

The nurse smiled and said "Mr Reed, if you are starting your dying process you have a very long way to go. Your blood pressure is good, your temperature is good, your blood sugar is normal, your circulation is good and you coloring is good. I don't think you need to worry too much about dying tonight."

I felt like an idiot. I did tell her that he had been extremely restless all day—agitated with his breathing. She told me to go to the refrigerator and bring her the package of medications.

She instructed me to give him the medication for "restlessness." Two pills every four hours.

"They will relax him and ease his restlessness" she promised.

These pills immediately quieted him down and put him into almost a "coma state".

After the nurse left Cheryl and I just sat there in total confusion.

"Am I really nuts, Cheryl?

"No Jacci, you are not. I have sat here with you and I have witnessed with you how Ron is. I don't know what really just happened, but I do know that wasn't the man that was here all night with us. Do you want me to stay the night with you?"

"No, I will be fine. And obviously so will Ron."

I slept like a baby that night. Knowing that the nurse believed Ron was far from his dying process, allowed me to relax and get some much needed rest.

I woke to Ron becoming restless and so I continued to give him two of his restlessness pills every four hours that night. Almost immediately after giving them to him, he would calm down and go back into a deep sleep.

Chapter XXII

The Last Day

Saturday, October 18th, 2003. Ron's sister, Kelly, and brother in law, Chuck, and nephews Zak and Nicholas were coming to visit.

That morning I woke Ron up, washed him and made him comfortable in his chair. He was awake but not really alert. Chuck and the boys stayed with Ron while Kelly and I went for breakfast.

The idea was for Chuck and the boys to visit with Ron for a while and Kelly was going to get me "out of the house" for a few hours. As we were finishing breakfast Kelly asked "So what do you want to do? Do you want to go shopping?"

"Kelly, I think we should go home. I really think I just want to go home".

We were only gone an hour. When we came home, Chuck said Ron had not moved the entire time we were gone. Kelly went into to talk to him. He did not respond. She held his hand but there was no reaction.

"Ron" she said "It's Kelly. Your sister. Talk to me. I came to see you. Can you hear me? Squeeze my hand if you can hear me".

Ron tried to open his eye but only half opened it, as if to say just let me be. We sat in the kitchen for over an hour waiting. Finally it was as though we heard a "tone" very low of harps or angelic music over the baby monitor. Perhaps we were hearing things. What was it? Kelly went back into the bedroom. Over the baby monitor I heard her now telling Ron it was okay to leave. Kelly called for me. Ron's breathing was 50 seconds apart now.

My last gift to Ron was to let him die at home. I did not realize that in return he would also be giving me a last gift. A gift of learning the beautiful transition of life into death. A gift of knowing that we are not alone in this world nor are we alone in the next. A gift of knowing that death does not have to be scary or fearing or sad.

I sat holding Ron's hand knowing he would die within five minutes. His breathing was almost 50 seconds apart now and he was in a coma like state. I sat and waited. Another breath. Was this the last one? Holding his hand I told him once more "It's just too hard, isn't it Ron? You want to go, don't you? It's okay Honey, you can go. I'll be okay, I promise. I love you,

I will always love you—now and forever". He drew his last breath. It was quiet and peaceful. There was no movement, not even a twitch. It was over. From my hands into the hands of God his spirit flew. He was safe and whole again and for that I was happy.

Goodbye my Ron—until we meet again . . .

Share your thoughts and reflections on this book with me.

Email be at:

Jaccismithreed@aol.com

And every day may you find the strength to continue to "Live Well, Laugh Often and Love Much."